THE ARAN ISLANDS

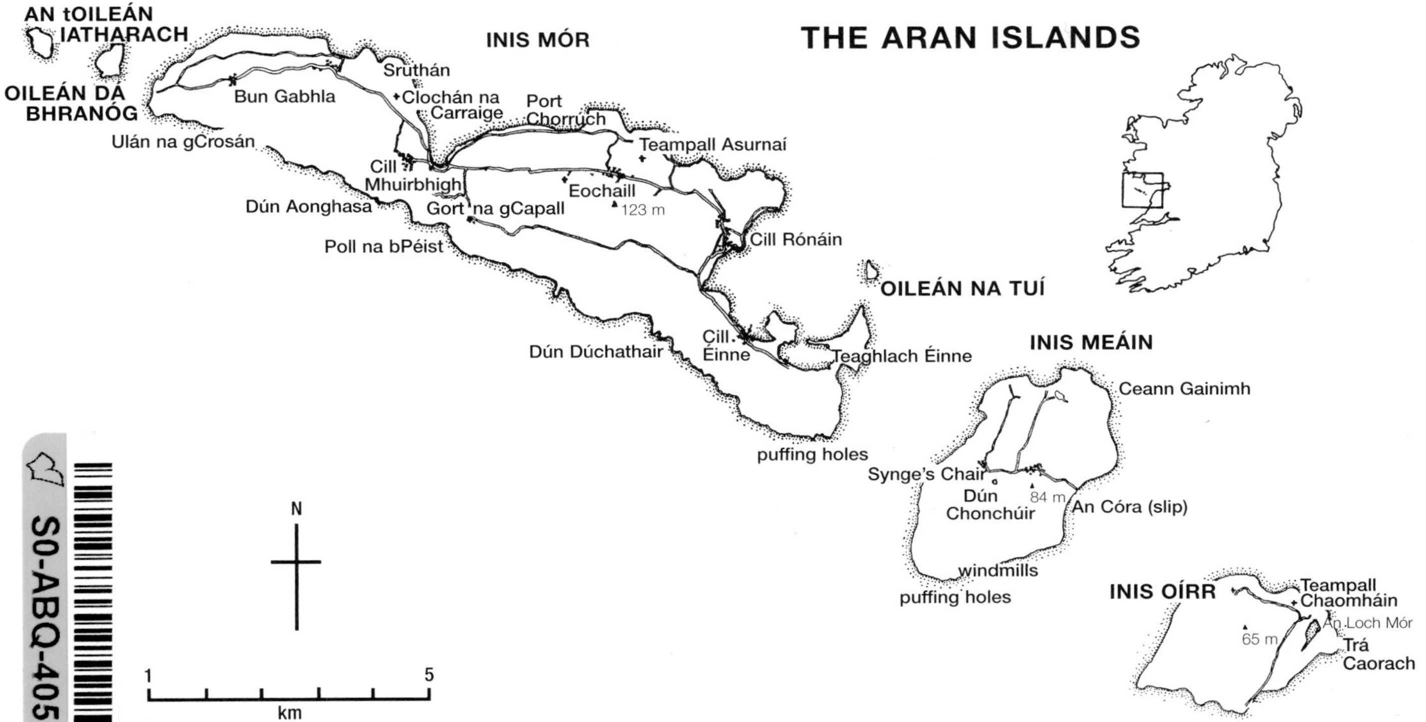

Ordnance Survey of Ireland Permit No. MP 006305 © Ordnance Survey Ireland/Government of Ireland

AN tOILEÁN IATHARACH

OILEÁN DA BHRANÓG

INIS MÓR

Ullán na gCrosán

Bun Gabhla

Dún Aonghasa

Poll na bPéist

Cill Mhuirbhigh

Gort na gCapall

Sruthán

Clochán na Carraige

Port Chorrúch

Eochaill
▲123 m

Teampall Asurnaí

Dún Dúchathair

Cill Éinne

Cill Rónáin

puffing holes

Teaghlach Éinne

OILEÁN NA TUÍ

Synge's Chair

Dún Chonchúir
▲84 m

An Córa (slip)

puffing holes

windmills

INIS MEÁIN

Ceann Gainimh

INIS OIRR

▲65 m

Teampall Chaomháin

Ag Loch Mór

Trá Caorach

N

km

1

5

Nature Guide
to the
Aran Islands

Na Blátha Craige

Adúirt mé leis na blátha:
    'Nach suarach an áit a fuair sibh
    Le bheith ag déanamh aeir
    Teannta suas anseo le bruach na haille
    Gan fúibh ach an chloch ghlas
    Agus salachar na n-éan
    Áit bhradach, lán le ceo
    Agus farraige cháite
    Ní scairteann grian anseo
    Ó Luan go Satharn
    Le gliondar a chur oraibh.'

Adúirt na blátha craige:
    'Is cuma linn, a stór,
    Táimid faoi dhraíocht
    Ag ceol na farraige.'

Liam O'Flaherty

Thrift (Sea Pink) at Synge's Chair, Inis Meáin

Nature Guide
to the
Aran Islands

CON O'ROURKE

THE LILLIPUT PRESS • DUBLIN

First published 2006 by
The Lilliput Press
62–63 Sitric Road, Arbour Hill
Dublin 7, Ireland
www.lilliputpress.ie

ISBN 1 84351 078 2

A CIP record for this title is available
from The British Library.

10 9 8 7 6 5 4 3 2 1

Front cover: View to the south-east of the three Aran Islands.
Dún Aonghasa (Inis Mór) in foreground; The Burren and
Cliffs of Moher (County Clare) in distance.

Institute of Biology Ireland

Typeset in 11pt Garamond
Cover design, text design and typesetting by Anú Design, Tara
Printed in England by MPG Books, Bodmin, Cornwall

An
Chomhairle
Oidhreachta

The
Heritage
Council

This publication has received support from The Heritage Council
under the 2006 Publications Grants Scheme.

Contents

Foreword

It gives me great pleasure to write the foreword for this beautiful publication, especially since Dr O'Rourke and I were fellow graduate students at Cornell University during the 1960s. It brings together in a single volume the forces of nature (geology, climate, flora, fauna and agriculture) that define the unique heritage of Aran, an extension of the renowned Burren in County Clare. Its appeal is broad-based, aimed both at casual visitors and those interested in natural history. It should also comprise a useful reference source for the various organizations involved in the islands' development. The guide is copiously illustrated, mostly with the author's own photographs. On a recent visit to the Royal Society of Antiquaries of Ireland, Merrion Square, on the occasion of their Presidential Lecture, I had the opportunity and pleasure to admire the striking photographs of the Irish countryside that Con O'Rourke has taken over the years.

Science has recently made a welcome return to our primary schools, as part of the government priority to increase public awareness of the vital role that science plays in national development. The series of scientific lectures and field forays in Aran organized by Dr O'Rourke and his colleagues for trainee primary teachers over the past twenty years should serve as a model for future teachers in interpreting their local natural environment for their pupils.

The author spent more than forty years as a research scientist in agriculture and was involved in the science awareness and youth programmes of the Institute of Biology of Ireland, the Royal Dublin Society and the Royal Irish Academy. He has applied his considerable experience and expertise to producing this comprehensive guide on the natural heritage of this truly unique and magnificent area.

Armed with the knowledge contained in this publication, the natural heritage of Aran is accessible to a wider audience and this will lead to a far greater appreciation of the need to ensure that the natural heritage of this unique area is safeguarded for future generations. Again let me congratulate Dr O'Rourke on the production of this lovely publication.

Dr Tom O'Dwyer, Chair
The Heritage Council/An Chomhairle Oidhreachta

Acknowledgments

NUI Dublin: Gerard Doyle, Emer Ní Cheallaigh, Ian Somerville; NUI Cork: Ken Bond; NUI Galway: Ronan Browne, Micheline Sheehy Skeffington, Robert Wilkes; Trinity College Dublin: Paddy Cunningham, Shane Mawe; University of Limerick: John Breen; Galway-Mayo Institute of Technology: David McGrath; Royal Dublin Society Library: Mary Kelleher, Ger Whelan; Dublin Naturalists' Field Club: Con Breen, Deirdre Hardiman, David Nash; Arramara Teoranta: Tony Barrow; Galway County Council: Kevin Finnerty; Botanic Gardens, Dublin: Matthew Jebb and (formerly) Maura Scannell; Met Éireann: Tom Sheridan; Geological Survey of Ireland: Andrew Sleeman; Fáilte Ireland; Ireland West Tourism; BirdWatch Ireland; Foras na Gaeilge; Department of the Environment, Heritage and Land Government; Áine de Blacam, Inis Meáin; Roger and Angela Faherty, Inis Meáin; Mícheál Ó Conaill, Inis Mór; Bríd Póil, Inis Óirr; Aisling Nic An tSithigh; Peter and Mary Carvill; Brendan Dunford; and Ruairí Ó hEithir

Permissions:
'Na Blátha Craige' by Liam O'Flaherty, by kind permission of Sáirséal – Ó Marcaigh and Caoimhín Ó Marcaigh
'Cuimhne an Domhnaigh' and 'An tEarrach Thiar' by Máirtín Ó Direáin, by kind permission of An Clóchomhar
'Ireland with Emily' by John Betjeman, by kind permission of John Murray Publishers
'Inis Meáin, Seanchas agus Scéalta' by Peadar Ó Concheanainn, by kind permission of An Gúm

'The Aran Islands' by Daphne Pochin Mould, by kind permission of David & Charles

'Lovers on Aran' by Seamus Heaney, by kind permission of the author

'The Death of Irish' by Aidan Mathews, by kind permission of the author

Illustration credits:

1.1 ERA-Maptec Ltd

2.1–2.3 by Helen Mathews

3.10, 3.44 by Con Breen

4.1–4.16 by Richard T. Mills

4.17–4.33 by Deirdre Hardiman

5.17 by Paul Kay, copyright Sherkin Island Marine Station

6.3 by Matt Nolan

All other photographs by the author.

Nature Guide
to the
Aran Islands

Introduction

The Aran Islands have been aptly described as one of the most written-about places in Ireland. This isolated rocky world midway up the west coast and at the north-western edge of Europe holds a particular fascination and appeals to a variety of interests. Most of the published works deal with the language (Irish/Gaelic), literature, social history, folklore and archaeology of the islands. Robert Flaherty's classic documentary film *Man of Aran* brought island life to the world's attention in the 1930s.

Some of the many books on the Aran Islands include brief sections on their natural history, i.e. their flora, fauna and geology. This *Nature Guide* goes into greater detail on these and related topics, and aims to encourage visitors to linger, learn and perhaps return.

It is only in recent decades that Aran's unique natural history has received official recognition. Some of the Aran rock formations, grasslands and marshes were classified by An Foras Forbartha in the 1970s as Areas of Scientific Interest (ASIs) of International, National or Local importance. On the basis of their unique flora, fauna and local environment, all three islands were later included in Natural Heritage Areas (NHAs). The large expanses of bare limestone currently comprise a Special Area of Conservation (SAC).

The impressive rock formations, the unique Burren-type flora thriving in what appears to be a barren 'lunar' landscape, the birds, the insects and the seashore life are of particular interest to that ever-increasing species, the eco-tourist.

The Aran Islands are a fragmented reef of the renowned Burren region of north-west County Clare, forming a breakwater across the mouth of Galway Bay. The geology, climate and farming practices of this elemental

3

and fascinating region determine its unique natural environment. Thus, although the islands physically and environmentally belong to the wider Burren region of County Clare (Munster province), they are in County Galway (Connaught province) in terms of civil and church administration, Irish-language dialect and sporting loyalties.

The islands cover 43.3 km² (4330 hectares), with a total population of 1280 in 2002 (compared to more than 3000 throughout most of the nineteenth century). Only about a third of the land can be farmed, with the rest comprising bare limestone rock or minimal rough grazing. A visitor's main impression is of a maze of stone walls (totalling 2400 km in length) enclosing small, irregularly shaped fields.[6.1]

The islands are named Inis Mór, Inis Meáin and Inis Oírr, meaning the big island, the middle island and the east island, respectively. The origin of the name Aran is disputed, but is most likely to be from the Irish for kidney (*ára*), meaning, in the case of Inis Mór at least, a kidney-shaped ridge of land (see map at front). To distinguish them from the islands of Arranmore (County Donegal) and Arran in Scotland, they have often been called 'The South Isles of Aran'. The islanders themselves often confine the word *Árann* to only the largest island, Inis Mór (also known as Aranmore). Since the islands are a Gaeltacht (Irish-speaking) area, all placenames in this *Nature Guide*, including the map, are in Irish, in accordance with the Placenames (*Ceantair Ghaeltachta*) Order 2004.

Although the Aran Islands and the wider Burren region are regarded as areas of elemental and timeless natural environment, their physical appearance today owes as much to man's influence as to other factors over thousands of years. At the end of the last Ice Age about 10,000 years ago, plants recolonized the land. The pioneer vegetation comprised scrub woodland (dominated, in turn, by Juniper, willow, birch, pine and Hazel) on a thin cover of glacial drift soil. Early farmers cleared the woodland, starting from about 4000 BC in The Burren and somewhat later in Aran. A combination of farming practices and climatic changes over the years led to soil erosion and the extensive bare limestone karst landscape of today. The presence of so many impressive Bronze Age (2000–600 BC) forts, such as Dún Aonghasa on Inis Mór[1.2] and Dún Chonchúir on Inis Meáin, suggests that the islands were once sufficiently fertile and prosperous to have supported a much larger population than that of today.

The Gaelic Revival of the late nineteenth century came to regard the

Aran Islands as a pure and untarnished bastion of ancient Irish tradition. Many antiquarians, linguists and writers went there for study, inspiration or reflection. Before long, as Tim Robinson wryly observed, 'the islands were in a perpetual state of being investigated' (1995). Early visitors included George Petrie and John O'Donovan, followed by William Wilde, Samuel Ferguson, Thomas Westropp, Eugene O'Curry, Eoin McNeill, Fr Eoghan O'Growney, Kuno Meyer, W.B. Yeats, Lady Gregory, Patrick Pearse, J.M. Synge, Seamus Delargy and James Joyce.

The British Association for the Advancement of Science (BAAS) met in Ireland for their 1857 annual meeting and the programme included a study tour of Aran by seventy members of their Ethnological Section. These formidable savants, led by the president of the Section, Sir William Wilde, held their annual general meeting and banquet within the prehistoric Dún Aonghasa fort,[1,2] with speeches in Irish, English and French, and dancing to bagpipes. Bemused islanders viewed the proceedings from the top of the ramparts.

Both the Anthropological Section of the BAAS and the Irish Ethnography Committee of the Royal Irish Academy (Haddon 1893) selected Aran for special study in the 1890s, as its inhabitants were considered to be racially and culturally the most representative of the original Celtic peoples. However, in the 1950s there was some dismay when newly available data on Irish ABO/rhesus blood groups showed that the Aran islanders were significantly *less* 'Celtic' than the Connaught norm. Furthermore, recent DNA analyses carried out by Trinity College Dublin throw doubts on the supposed dominant Celtic strain in the overall Irish population.

Probably the first scientific visitor to Aran was the Welsh naturalist and Celticist Edward Lhwyd in 1700. However, systematic study of the islands' natural environment dates only from the mid-nineteenth century. The flora, fauna and geology of Inis Mór were studied by Queen's College Galway (now NUI Galway) and the Geological Survey in 1864. In 1895 the Irish Field Club Union organized a botanical foray on Inis Mór, led by Robert Lloyd Praeger. Since then a regular stream of scientists and students have studied the natural history of the islands.

Improved sea and air access to the islands has increased the number of visitors (mostly day-trippers) to approximately 200,000 per annum. Tourism has now replaced fishing and farming as the main economic activity. Increased tourism, however, inevitably affects the natural environment.

The sandy coastal areas (machairs) of the islands are rich in flora and birdlife but are particularly vulnerable to damage by visitors. Even the hard limestone karst is not immune to incessant human traffic.

The entire flora and fauna of the Aran Islands comprises thousands of species and to describe them all is obviously beyond the scope of this *Nature Guide*. However, most of the plants, rock types, birds, insects and seashore species typical of Aran, and which visitors are likely to see, are included. More detailed information can be sourced from the bibliography.

This *Nature Guide* derives from the courses and field forays on Aran's natural history organized by the author for the Institute of Biology of Ireland since the early 1980s. They were designed for tourists on cultural/ environmental weekends, for second-level students on Irish-language summer courses, and for trainee primary teachers on their three-week Gaeltacht stints. As an aid to the courses, a bilingual video on Aran geology, climate, flora and birdlife was produced by the Institute in 1991, followed in 1993 by a poster on the local flora, *Blátha Árann*. With the very welcome reintroduction of a Social, Environmental and Scientific module into the primary-school curriculum, the video, poster and this *Nature Guide* should serve as a useful model for teachers in interpreting the environment of their local areas.

The heritage of the Aran Islands is a unique but fragile combination of the Irish language, folklore, social history, archaeology, natural environment and traditional farming. Its natural environment, particularly its Burren-type flora, reflects current land-use practices. However, overall development of the islands' economy will inevitably affect all aspects of their heritage. For this reason, the future development and maintenance of the islands' tourism, natural environment and farming sectors requires sensitive management and coordination for their mutual benefit and long-term survival.

Geology

1

Mórchuid chloch is gannchuid cré
(Much rock and little soil)

Máirtín Ó Direáin, 'Cuimhne an Domhnaigh'

Stony seaboard, far and foreign
Stony hills poured over space
Stony outcrops of the Burren
Stones in every fertile place

John Betjeman, 'Ireland with Emily'

In geological and botanical terms The Burren (from *Boireann*, 'a rocky place') is defined as the approximately 300 km^2 of karstic limestone of north Clare, south-east Galway and the Aran Islands. It is one of the largest stretches of exposed limestone in Europe. In the satellite image[1.1] the bare grey limestone of Aran and The Burren can be clearly distinguished.

Geology is the study of 'the bones of the earth' and nowhere in Ireland are these bones more visible than in the Aran Islands. Limestone is Ireland's commonest rock, laid down on the seabed from animal and plant remains in the Carboniferous Period. Geologically and botanically, the sedimentary limestone terrain of The Burren and Aran differs quite markedly from that of the igneous granites and metamorphic rocks of nearby Connemara on the opposite side of Galway Bay.

With the melting of the ice about 10,000 years ago, at the end of the last Ice Age, sea levels gradually rose by about 100 m. This not only created the island of Ireland but also separated the Aran Islands from the limestone mass of The Burren. They are the only limestone islands of any significant size off the Irish and British coasts.

The Aran limestone is composed mainly of calcium carbonate, with dolomite (calcium magnesium carbonate) occurring in the darker strata. Limestone is more easily worked than granite and slabs for gravestones were regularly exported to Connemara (often in exchange for peat fuel). It

1.1 Satellite image of Galway Bay. The bare limestone karst of the Aran Islands and The Burren (centre right) appears light grey

9

was also exported in the form of lime for mortar and whitewash, and to 'sweeten' the acid soils of Connemara. The ruins of a lime kiln can be seen at Cill Éinne pier on Inis Mór.

The geology of The Burren and Aran has two main features:

1. Solid geology: Limestone from the Lower Carboniferous Period (formed more than 300 million years ago)
2. Glacial geology: Glacial 'erratics' and boulder clay left behind after the relatively recent Ice Age of the Quaternary Period (1,700,000 to 10,000 years ago)

Solid geology

The universe was created, according to the latest evidence, 13.7 billion years ago (BYA) during the 'Big Bang'. Our own solar system dates from about 4.5 BYA, with life on earth starting about 3.5 BYA. On a geological timescale, the Aran rocks are not particularly ancient. To be tediously precise, they are from the Burren and Slievenaglasha formations of the upper part (Halkerian/Asbian/Brigantian) of the Viséan Stage of the Lower Carboniferous Period (Palaeozoic Era) of 345–325 million years ago (MYA) (Pracht *et al.* 2004). The oldest rocks in Ireland, dating from about 1750–1800 MYA (Precambrian Period), are on Inishtrahull off Malin Head, County Donegal, and on the Mullet peninsula, County Mayo.

The Aran limestone was formed by deposition on the seabed of the remains of various marine life forms. Each metre depth of Aran limestone would represent some tens of thousands of years of such deposition. This occurred not in its current position but at the bottom of a warm shallow sea near the equator. At that time what are now northern Europe, Greenland, North America and much of Asia were joined in a single land-mass (Laurasia). Movements of the earth's major tectonic plates have been continuous over geological time and about 270 MYA (Permian Period) the limestone drifted some thousands of kilometres northwards to its present position and rose above sea level in places.

The many animal and plant fossils[1.8 1.9] in the Aran rocks are of tropical species from the Carboniferous Period, requiring a minimum annual temperature of 18°C. These were mostly primitive species, i.e. long before the

1.2 Cliff face at Dún Aonghasa, Inis Mór, showing two clay wayboard strata in the limestone

evolution of birds, dinosaurs and mammals. However, some fish species from the Carboniferous Period, such as sharks and coelacanths, survive relatively unchanged to the present.

The Aran Islands rise to a maximum of 123 m above Galway Bay. The limestone bedding planes[1.2] are almost horizontal, dipping 1–3° to the south. The limestone has been weathered into terraces, separated by escarpments 2–10 m high, giving a tiered or stepped appearance to the Galway Bay side of the three islands.[1.3] The terraces comprise relatively hard limestone layers, separated by narrow and softer clay layers,[1.10] which originated from a succession of changes in sea level.

The clay layers underlying each limestone terrace are defined as 'clay wayboards' (though often described as 'shales') and represent fossil soil horizons. There was sufficient time for these soil horizons to form over the limestone before sea levels rose and deposition resumed. The clay layers are more susceptible to weathering and erosion, leading to undercutting and eventual collapse of the overhanging limestone strata. Erosion of the clay has also created the numerous caves on the islands, with their associated legends of underground passages between the ancient forts, and even between the islands. The alternating layers of limestone and clay are seen to best advantage in the cliffs rising to 70 m on the south-western side of

Inis Mór. Here, the erosion of the clay results in horizontal grooves and ledges between the limestone layers.[1.2]

Looking south-east across Galway Bay from Aran, a continuation of the distinct layers of limestone bedding planes that occur on Aran is visible on the Burren hills.[1.4] Their contemporaneous origin is confirmed by the similarity of their fossils and limestone composition. The Burren strata dip gently south-south-west towards Doolin, where they run under the younger (Upper Carboniferous) sandstones and shales of the Cliffs of Moher.[6.2] There is little folding or deformation of the strata in Aran, except for relatively minor faults at Poll na Brioscarnach, Maoilín an Ghrióra and a few other places on Inis Mór. This contrasts with the folding of some of the limestone hills in The Burren, such as the well-known and striking syncline at Mullach Mór.

Karst, clints and grykes

In geological terms, the Aran landscape is defined as a 'glaciated karst', the term 'karst' deriving from the Serbo-Croat *krs* and the Slovenian *kras* for an area of stony bare ground in what is now a part of Croatia and Slovenia (Daly *et al.* 2000). It is characterized by flat slabs of bare limestone, called

1.3 Limestone terraces, Inis Meáin

1.4 Limestone karst of Aran (foreground) and The Burren, County Clare (distance); **1.5** Clints and grykes, Inis Mór

smooth pavement or clints, interspersed with deep cracks called grykes.[1.5] The most dominant gryke system runs south-south-west, with a less-developed secondary system at right angles to it. The vertical grykes (called *scailp* in Irish, as in The Scalp defile in the Dublin mountains) are usually straight and, combined with the horizontal bedding of the limestone, give a smooth, blocky ('chocolate-bar') structure to the landscape. This pattern is best seen in the perfectly rectangular, swimming-pool sized (33 x 12 m) Poll na bPéist (The Pool of the Sea Serpents) in Inis Mór.[1.6] Tim Robinson (1986) has contrasted the striking oblong/cuboid rock structure of Aran with the more rounded 'natural' landscape of most other parts of Ireland.

The clints often contain narrow white bands of calcite (calcium carbonate)[1.7] and dark bands of chert (an amorphous form of silicon dioxide). The calcite bands were deposited from hot aqueous solutions that were forced up through planes of weakness in the limestone. The clints may also be weathered into a jumble of loose slabs ('shattered pavement'), which when walked on produce distinctive sounds varying from grunts to musical tinklings.

The grykes originated from joints caused by lateral tensions in the limestone when the Atlantic Ocean was being formed. The joints were subsequently enlarged to 10–100 cm wide, and up to 6 m deep, over thousands of years by the dissolving action of rainwater. Delicate plants that are sensitive to frost, wind and salt-spray (such as Maidenhair Fern[3.45]) thrive in the grykes.

In their passage through the air, raindrops absorb carbon dioxide gas to form a weak acid (carbonic acid), a natural 'acid rain'. This acid dissolves the normally insoluble limestone (calcium carbonate) to form soluble

1.6 Rectangular rock pool, Poll na bPéist, Inis Mór

1.7 Calcite band in limestone, Inis Meáin

calcium bicarbonate, which drains away with the rainwater, as shown by
the following formulae:

$$H_2O \text{ (rainwater)} + CO_2 \text{ (carbon dioxide)} \rightarrow H_2CO_3 \text{ (carbonic acid)}$$

$$H_2CO_3 \text{ (carbonic acid)} + CaCO_3 \text{ (limestone, insoluble)} \rightarrow Ca(HCO_3)_2$$
$$\text{(calcium bicarbonate, soluble)} + H_2O \text{ (water)}$$

Geologists estimate that the flat surfaces of the limestone clints are being
dissolved at a rate of about 0.05 mm per annum in The Burren and at a
somewhat slower rate in Aran, leading some alarmists to predict that eventually the islands may dissolve away completely. Where the limestone clints
are protected from rainwater, however, there is less dissolution and the surface
can be visibly higher (stepped) than the surrounding exposed rock. These
steps or pedestals can be seen under glacial erratics (described below)[1.13]
and were measured at 6.3–10 cm high in the first geological survey of Aran in
1866. Pedestals also occur under the oldest stone walls, known from the first
Ordnance Survey maps to have been in place since at least the early 1800s.

The acid rainwater, in addition to expanding the grykes, also dissolves
out solution runnels (rinnenkarren) and small hollows (kamenitzas) in the

1.8 Fossils (brachiopod shells) in Aran limestone

flat clints. These depressions hold rainwater in which a distinctive jelly-like cyanobacterium (*Nostoc* spp.) grows.[3.66] The *Nostoc* itself also produces an acid that further enlarges the solution hollows.

Fossils

The Aran limestone is rich in fossils, originating 345–325 MYA in the warm seas of the Carboniferous Period. As you ascend the limestone strata some of the fossil species present are replaced by others higher up the evolutionary chain. Certain fossils may be unique to particular strata and thus can be used for relative dating and correlation between the Aran and Burren limestones.

The Aran fossils[1.8][1.9] include gastropods, corals, foraminifera, crinoids (sea lilies), conodonts (extinct early vertebrates) and brachiopods (Daly 1977; Pracht *et al.* 2004). A wide selection of these, including a shark's tooth, is on display in Ionad Árann, the Heritage Centre on Inis Mór.

Water

Water shortages occur regularly in Aran, particularly in the summer tourist season. Fortunately for the islands, the clay wayboards under the limestone terraces[1.10] are of low permeability and serve to trap rainwater. Without them, water would percolate swiftly down to sea level through the fissured

Clockwise from top: **1.9** Fossils in Aran limestone (left: Gastropod snail; right: Chaetetid sponge); **1.10** Clay wayboard layer under limestone terrace, Inis Meáin; **1.11** The old and the new. Rain collector (early twentieth century) and windmills powering desalination plant, Inis Meáin

limestone, making the islands uninhabitable for man or beast. Most of the islands' wells flow from the wayboards, many of which have now been tapped for the public water supply. In fields remote from wells or a piped supply, rainwater-collecting cisterns provide water for livestock.[1.11] Their construction was promoted by the Congested Districts Board in the early twentieth century, and later by the Department of Agriculture.

As most of the accessible and productive wells in Aran have now been tapped, alternative sources of water have had to be found. The first windmill-powered desalination plant in Ireland was installed on Inis Meáin in 2002.[1.11] The windmills generate electricity which, via a vacuum distillation process, converts seawater into fresh water to augment the public supply.

1.12 Stream at Sruthán, Inis Mór

Aran and The Burren are remarkable for the almost complete absence of permanent rivers or streams. Where wells occur at the base of clay layers, the water rapidly percolates through the fissured limestone to re-emerge at the next clay layer and so on stepwise down to sea level (karstic drainage). The only surface watercourse of any consequence in The Burren is the Caher river between Black Head and Fanore. In Aran there are no rivers at all and only a few small and seasonal streams, such as at the eponymous Sruthán ('stream' in Irish) on Inis Mór, which practically dries up in summer.[1.12] Inis Meáin has a few small streams, trickling for only short distances before disappearing underground.

Glacial geology

Erratics

Scattered incongruously around the Aran landscape are large boulders, known as 'glacial erratics'.[1.13] They are so-called because they are often not of limestone and are thus unrelated to the local geology. They were deposited during two main stages (the Munsterian and the Midlandian) in the Ice Age. During the last (Midlandian) cold stage (70,000 to 10,000 years ago) a large glacier centred on Connemara dragged rocks from there as far south as Cork. When the ice melted, the rocks were dumped on the local landscape. Most of the large erratics in Aran are of Connemara granite from the Maamturk mountains, or of conglomerate. They are called *carraigreacha Chonamara* (Connemara boulders) by the islanders. Smaller sandstone specimens from Oughterard (near Lough Corrib) are also found in the stone walls and an impressive 'swarm' of large limestone erratics can be seen between Iaráirne and the south-east tip of Inis Mór.

The granite erratics are harder than limestone and have been used locally as *bullán* (or *ballán*) stones. A *bullán* is a hollowed-out stone, often associated with monastic sites where they were used as bowls, as mortars for crushing grain and shellfish, or as holy water fonts. The term is also used for small seashore rock pools. The granite *bullán* set inside the road wall at the Inis Meáin church,[1.14] serving as a holy-water font, was moved from the nearby late-medieval Teampall Mhuire when the new church was built in 1939.

Glacial drift

The Ice Age glaciers contained a mixture of large boulders (erratics) together with stones, sand and finer materials (boulder clay), collectively known as glacial drift. It is likely that Aran and The Burren were once covered with a layer of such glacial drift. This would have sustained a good plant cover, particularly of pine and Hazel woodland. However, due to erosion, and possibly tree-felling and other agricultural practices, this original soil cover has been much depleted. A climatic deterioration starting about 5000 years ago would also have hastened erosion. Boulder clay now remains only in localized pockets in Aran, such as near Loch an Charra and Port Mhuirbhigh on Inis Mór, and at the airstrip on Inis Meáin. Calcifuge (lime-hating) plants, such as heather, may be found growing on the remnants of the boulder clay (Chapter 3).

Top: **1.13** Granite glacial erratic, Inis Meáin. Mosses and lichens are more prevalent on the sheltered (left) side of the boulder; Above: **1.14** Holy-water font (granite *bullán*), Inis Meáin church

Climate

2

… an gaoth aniar aneas a shéideas comh borbchoimhthíoch agus go mbeadh sí i gcruth na hadharca a bhaint de na ba. (… the south-west wind so fierce as to blow the horns off the cows.)

Peadar Ó Concheanainn, 'Inis Meáin, Seanchas agus Scéalta'

The climate of the Aran Islands, like that of most of the west coast of Ireland, is aptly classified as 'extreme Atlantic' or 'oceanic'. Situated off the north-west of the European mainland at 53°N, the islands are directly in the path of the rain-bearing Atlantic depressions. The waters of the North Atlantic Drift (a north-east extension of the Gulf Stream) bathe the west coast and maintain significantly higher winter temperatures than in other regions at similar latitudes. Compared with the Irish mainland, Aran has its own climate, characterized by mild winters, high winds, high relative humidity and moderately high rainfall. In the absence of local weather recording, the data for the Aran Islands shown in 2.1, 2.2 and 2.3 has been extrapolated from regional information.

Bright sunshine, at about 1300 hours per year, is significantly lower than the 1700 hours found near Rosslare in the south-east. However, this is compensated for by the high reflection of available sunshine from the rocks and seashore – causing unanticipated sunburn for unwary tourists.

Temperature

Aran's oceanic climate results in a smaller temperature range between summer highs and winter lows than occurs in Ireland's interior. The mean air temperature in July in Aran is 15°C. This is similar to that in other coastal areas – such as those of Galway and Mayo – but is lower than the 16°C found in inland areas of the south-east, and around Dublin and Cork cities.

It is the winter temperatures that distinguish Aran from most of the rest of the country. The mean daily air temperature in January is between 6.5° and 7°C,[2.1] which is only about a degree lower than Rome for the same month. This is significantly higher than in the north Midlands (4–4.5°C) and is only exceeded in the Cork and Kerry peninsulas (above 7°C). The waters of the North Atlantic Drift surrounding the islands are about 9°C in January and help to moderate winter temperatures. Thus frost and snow are infrequent and rarely persist. Tourists from continental Europe and North America often remark on, and sometimes even photograph, the 'naked' (uninsulated) water tanks and pipes on the roofs of Aran houses.

Reflections from the rocks, sand and sea during sunny periods in winter can increase local air temperatures significantly. Direct sunlight on the limestone pavements (clints) raises their surface temperature by up to 8°C.

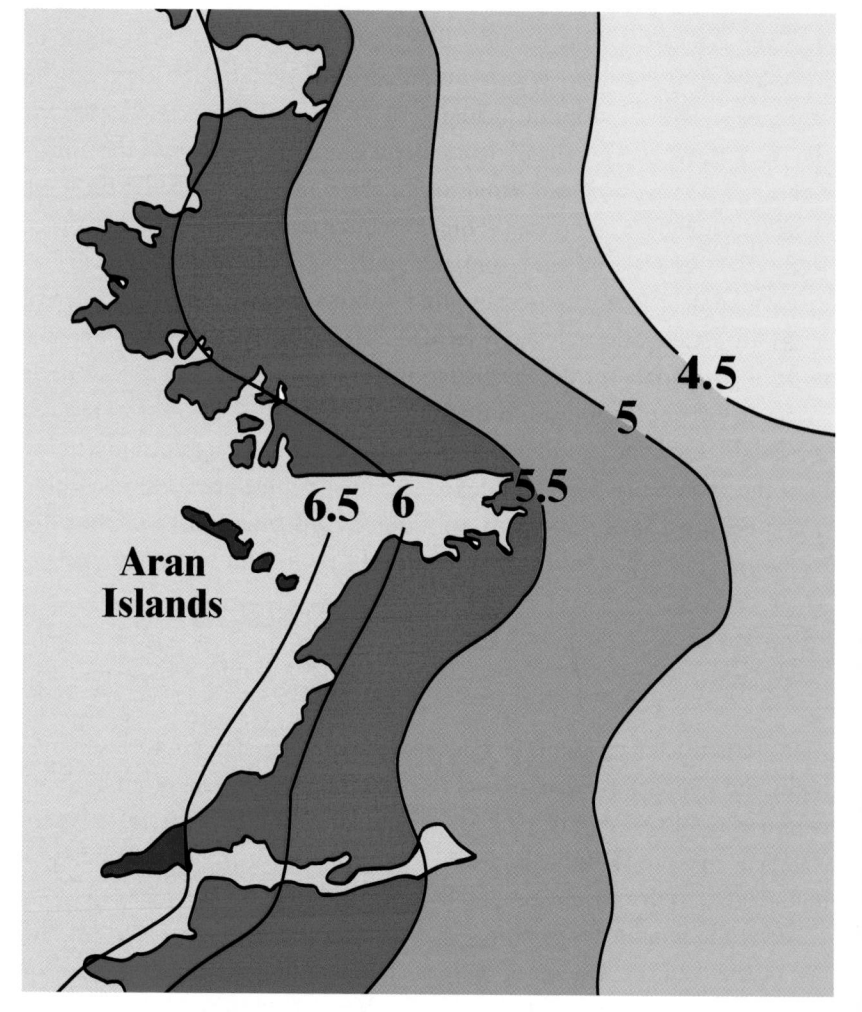

2.1 January isotherms (°C), West of Ireland (*Source: Met Éireann*)

In addition, the rock masses readily absorb sunlight energy and serve as natural storage heaters.

The minimum temperature for grass growth is about 6°C and this determines the system of livestock husbandry in Aran (Chapter 6). As mentioned above, the mean January temperature in Aran is above 6.5°C, so grass grows practically year-round and no winter housing is required for livestock. As the terrain is unsuited to mechanized silage production, traditional haymaking[6.3] and fodder roots provide any supplementary winter feeding required.

Wind

Robert Lloyd Praeger, one of Ireland's most renowned naturalists, described the winter climate of Ireland's exposed west coast as 'a succession of westerly gales with westerly winds between'. The mean annual wind speed in Aran is between 6 and 7 m/sec (Force 4, 26 kph),[2.2] nearly twice that of the south Midlands (below 4 m/sec). The persistent high winds, gusting to more than 150 kph in winter, regularly disrupt shipping to the islands. Prolonged bad weather during a winter in the 1980s delayed the landing of building materials for a new pier on the islands from Christmas until Easter. However, air services can resume once storms abate, in contrast to the ferries, which may have to wait a few days until sea conditions moderate.

Storms have caused many shipwrecks and lost lives over the centuries. The freighter *Plassey* was holed on Carraig na Finnise off Inis Oírr in a

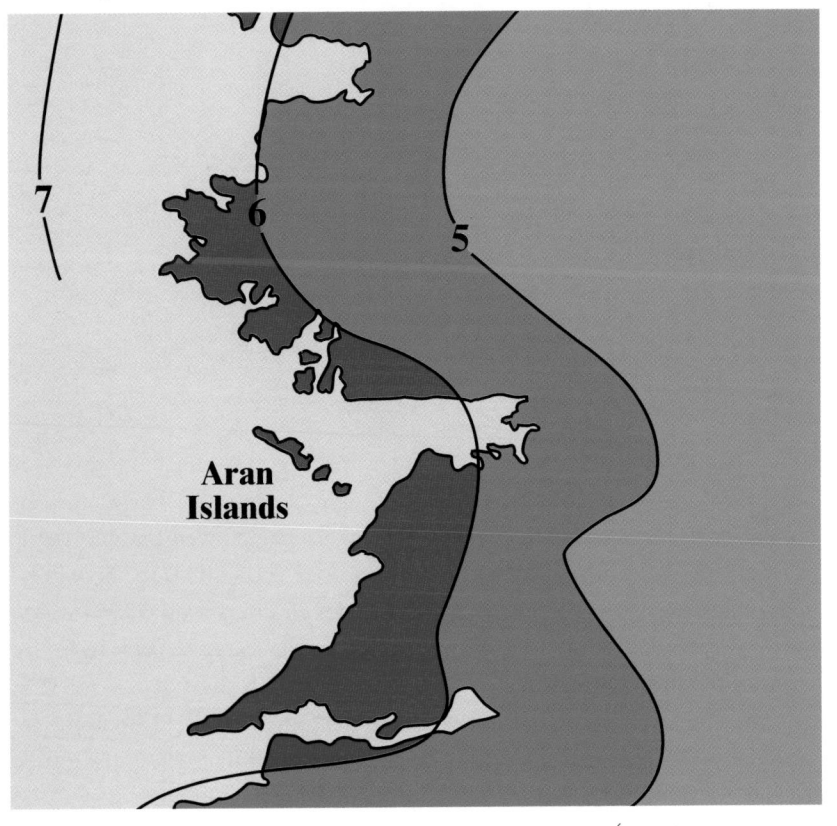

2.2 Mean annual windspeeds (m/sec), West of Ireland (*Source: Met Éireann*)

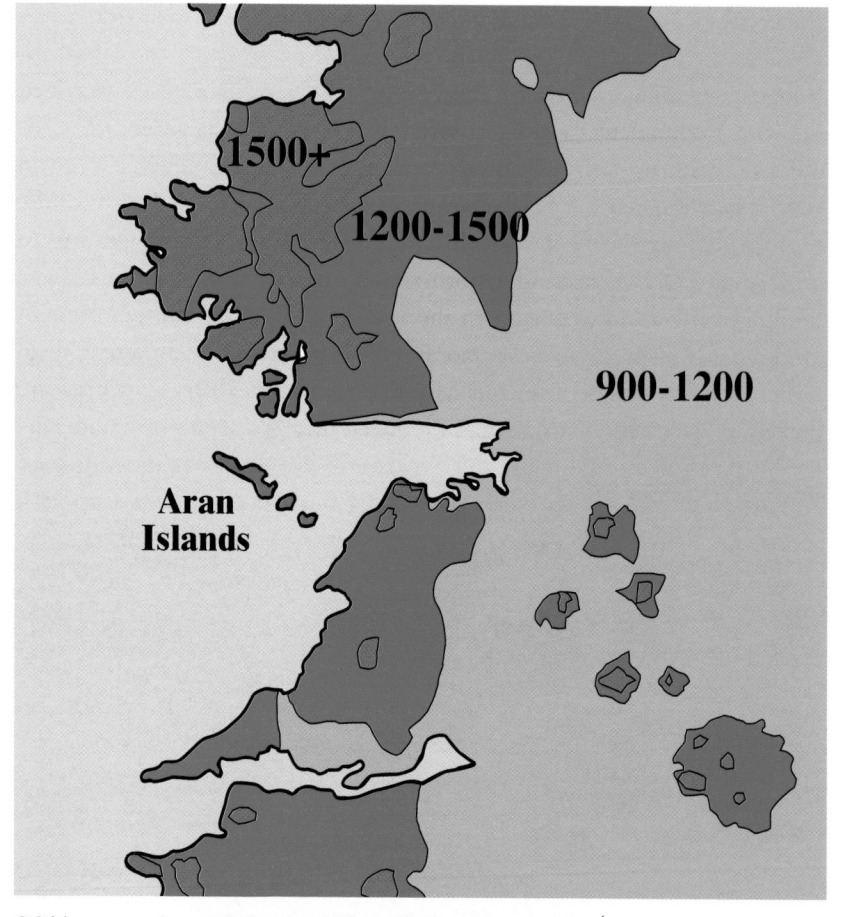

2.3 Mean annual precipitation (mm),West of Ireland (*Source: Met Éireann*)

south-easterly gale in 1960. It was swept ashore at Trá Caorach and over the years a succession of gales drove it above high-tide level.[2.4] The Aran fishermen are well aware of the sea's dangers, as in Synge's well-known quote: 'A man who is not afraid of the sea will soon be drownded, for he will be going out on a day he shouldn't. But we do be afraid of the sea, and we do only be drownded now and again.' Synge's play *Riders to the Sea* is based on an Aran boating tragedy.

The effects of high winds on plant life in Aran are stark. Trees are practically non-existent, apart from two small woods on Inis Mór.[3.2] Shrubs such as Hawthorn, Blackthorn and Juniper are deformed (wind-sculpted),[2.5] ground-hugging or can only survive in the lee of the stone walls. In addition to wind damage, salt spray in winter storms stunts plant growth and in particular scorches the pastures on the windward side of the islands. The salt spray also rapidly rusts vehicles and exposed ironwork.

The winter gales create impressive storm (block) beaches along the cliffs and terraces on the windward side of Inis Mór and Inis Meáin.[2.6 2.7] Huge stone blocks (megaclasts) are broken off the cliff tops and flung far back into jumbled ridges. An indication of the force of the waves can be seen on Inis Meáin where the storm beach, one of the highest in Ireland, reaches its limit of more than 50 m above sea level near Synge's Chair. Roderic O'Flaherty (1684) records an 'extraordinary inundation' in 1640, which swept right over a low-lying part of Inis Mór near Cill Mhuirbhigh. However, this may have been caused by a tsunami, generated by the north-west European

Clockwise from top left: 2.4 Wreck of the *Plassey*, Trá Caorach, Inis Oírr; 2.5 Wind-sculpted Hawthorn; 2.6 Storm beach, Inis Meáin

2.7 Storm beach on top of 40 m cliff, An tUlán Liath, Inis Meáin. Green alga (*Ulva*) on cliff face

earthquake of 4 April of that year, rather than by a conventional Atlantic storm.

Puffing holes are a feature of the cliffs and terraces to the south-west of Inis Mór and Inis Meáin. The wind-driven waves undercut the rock face and eventually break upwards some distance inland.[2.8] [2.9] Depending on wind strength and the state of the tide, the puffing holes 'emit prodigious columns of water to the height of a [sailing] ship's mast' (O'Flaherty 1824). The rectangular 33 x 12 m pool of Poll na bPéist (The Pool of the Sea Serpents) near Dún Aonghasa on Inis Mór[1.6] probably originated from a puffing hole.

Blowing sand is a persistent problem on the islands. On Inis Oírr, buildings are regularly engulfed and the sand has to be cleared out of Teampall Chaomháin each year before the saint's Pattern Day on 14 June. Marram grass has been planted to stabilize the dunes; its erect leaves slow the wind and its deep roots bind the sand.[3.62] On Inis Meáin, a road down-wind of the airstrip has been filled to the top of the stone walls with wind-blown sand.[2.10] In this case, the persistent wind blowing across the exposed airfield picks up sand on the way. The wind, together with its entrained sand, filters through the voids in the upwind wall of the road. Then, in the lee of the wall, the wind speed drops and the sand is deposited into the roadway.

On the positive side, Aran is an ideal site for harnessing wind energy. An experimental windmill was erected on Inis Oírr in the 1980s. On Inis Meáin three windmills were installed in 2002. These generate electricity for the island and also convert seawater into fresh water (by vacuum distillation) to augment the public supply.[1.11] Since 1997 electricity has been supplied from the national grid to the islands via underwater cables, allowing the flow to be reversed when wind-generated power on Inis Meáin is surplus to the island's requirements.

Rainfall

By west of Ireland standards, annual precipitation in Aran (falling almost entirely as rainfall) is moderate. It averaged 1128 mm per annum at Cill Rónáin in the 1931–60 period, about the same as for nearby mainland lowlands. Rain recording in Aran has since ceased but is now estimated to be at the lower end of the 1200–1500 mm per annum range.[2.3] Rain occurs on 175–200 days per annum, spread throughout the seasons, and usually as moderate falls rather than downpours. Rainfall is considerably higher on the hills in nearby Connemara and County Clare.[2.3]

Owing to the thin soil cover and the porous limestone bedrock, rainfall rapidly drains away and summer droughts are common. In contrast to tourists and mainland farmers, the Aran farmer prefers moderate rain at regular intervals during the summer. When horses were more prevalent, they were regularly transported by hookers (the local sailboats) to Connemara for the summer. This transhumance (seasonal movement of livestock) is graphically described in Synge's book *The Aran Islands*. Occasionally cattle also had to be included in the shipments. Tankers have been used to import water in particularly dry seasons.

In the early 1900s the Congested Districts Board promoted the building of large water-collecting troughs in fields remote from wells or a piped supply.[1.11] They were based on designs from arid countries, originally using the local flagstones but later concrete-built. The run-off from the roof of a barn or bothy (*cró*) could also be ducted into the troughs. The public water-supply systems on the islands have now tapped most of the useful wells and, with occasional rationing, they can survive most shortages. However, a large increase in tourism could result in regular water shortages.

Air quality

The air in Aran has travelled over some thousands of kilometres of the rainy Atlantic and has been 'scrubbed' of practically all pollutants originating from industrialized and populated areas. It is not surprising that Mace Head in nearby Connemara was chosen as the site for an international atmospheric research station (run by the Physics Department, NUI Galway) to investigate the pristine Atlantic air.

The most obvious indicator of the clean Aran air is the profuse growth of lichens and mosses on rocks and twigs. Lichens and mosses are particularly affected by sulphur dioxide pollution, as can be seen when their growth on limestone walls in Aran and a mainland city is compared.[3.63 3.64]

Clockwise from top left: 2.8 Puffing hole (quiescent phase), Inis Mór; 2.9 Puffing hole (active phase), Inis Meáin; 2.10 *Go n-éirí an bóthar leat!* (May the road rise with you!) Road filled with wind-blown sand, Inis Meáin

Flora

3

To walk the islands is to be continually delighted and surprised by their plants, bushes, and ferns.

Daphne Pochin Mould, 'The Aran Islands'

Overview

The Aran Islands are an extension of The Burren of County Clare and the two areas comprise a single 'biogeographic' region.[1.1 1.4] As already defined in Chapter 1, The Burren (from *Boireann*, 'a rocky place') comprises the approximately 300 km^2 of karstic limestone of north County Clare, southeast County Galway and the Aran Islands. This limestone largely determines the remarkable flora of the region, which is quite different from that on the granites and metamorphic rocks of nearby Connemara.

Aran and The Burren are one great rock garden that is never out of bloom. The greens, reds, yellows, purples and whites of the vegetation are particularly well set off by the matt grey backdrop of the limestone. Here can be found plants of Mediterranean–Atlantic and Arctic–Alpine affinities, all growing together near sea level. Plants typical of the Burren mainland in County Clare are also common in Aran. However, there are some notable exceptions; Mountain Avens (*Dryas octopetala*), though widespread in County Clare, is absent from Aran. On the other hand, Purple Milk-vetch[3.13] (*Astragalus danicus*) is found in Ireland only in Aran.

Although Aran and The Burren are home to about twenty-five species that are unknown or rare in the rest of Ireland, the normal range of plants common to unimproved grassland is also present. Though comprising less than 1 per cent of the land area of Ireland, three-quarters of the country's entire native flora can be found there. The Burren section of the Botanic Gardens in Dublin[3.1] is a creditable attempt at representing this unique habitat and topography. Massive limestone slabs (clints) have been laid down and the gaps in between (grykes, *scailp* in Irish) planted with typical Burren species. However, it is best to keep looking downwards, as the Burren illusion evaporates if one looks up and sees the luxurious foliage of the large trees in the immediate background.

As it would be impracticable to include the more than 400 plant species recorded in Aran in this *Nature Guide*, it does not aspire to being a complete flora of the islands. Apart from some notable rarities and oddities, the list is therefore limited to some sixty species that are particularly associated with Aran and The Burren, or those that are 'frequent' or 'abundant' and therefore likely to be noticed by the casual visitor. Well-known wild flowers and weeds that occur countrywide, such as daisies and dandelions, are omitted.

3.1 Burren section, Botanic Gardens, Dublin

Botanists in Aran

As part of The Burren, the Aran flora has been studied by botanists and enthusiastic amateurs for centuries. One of the first to visit was the Welsh botanist and Celticist Edward Lhwyd, who included Aran in his Irish tour in 1700 (Lhwyd 1712). However, systematic recording of the islands' flora did not begin until the mid-nineteenth century. L. Ogilby and W. Andrews made separate 'botanical rambles' in 1845, the latter noting that he was 'greeted with an assembly of rare and beautiful plants'. E.P. Wright recorded more than 150 species in Aran in 1866 (Wright 1866, 1867). This was followed by the first detailed survey (372 species) of all three islands by Henry Chichester Hart (1875). He noted: 'the astonishment shown by the shouts of the natives as I went over Inishmaan, marking down all the plants as I found them, seemed to imply that it had seldom been visited by any stranger'. A steady stream of botanists visited the islands from the mid- to late nineteenth century, culminating in a foray to Inis Mór in 1895 by the Irish Field Club Union (Praeger 1895).

The maze of high stone walls has been a great hindrance to all visiting botanists. Even the intrepid Hart, who possessed 'demonic energy', remarked that the walls 'are erected with no consideration for the shins of scientific explorers'. Nathaniel Colgan (1893), who noted 419 species and described the Aran flora as 'decidedly rich', solved the stone wall problem by employing a local boy to knock down and rebuild gaps as he went along.

Botanical activity in Aran waned in the first half of the twentieth century, due mainly to the disruptions caused by two World Wars and the establishment of the new Irish state. As Derek Mooney observed: 'The impoverished new State, confronting enormous political and social problems, had little interest in the natural environment' (Sterry 2004). This contrasted with Great Britain, where many enthusiastic professionals and amateurs had been recording local floras for centuries past.

Interest in the Aran flora revived from the late 1950s onwards, coinciding with greater public awareness of our environment and the inclusion of biology in the school curriculum. Individual forays were made by Con Breen, Cilian Roden and Tim Robinson, together with group forays from University College Dublin (J.J. Moore, J. White), Trinity College Dublin (D.A. Webb), An Foras Forbartha (R. Goodwillie), the Wildlife Service (T.G.F. Curtis), the Botanic Gardens (M.J.P. Scannell) and the Botanical Society of the British Isles. Professor Webb published a definitive flora of Aran in 1980, totalling some 437 species (Webb 1980). He later (with M.J.P. Scannell in 1983) published the *Flora of Connemara and The Burren*, in which the Aran Islands were included in their Region 2 of The Burren. A supplement to the *Flora* was published in 2000 (Scannell & Jebb 2000).

References to the natural history of Aran (particularly to the rocks and plants) crop up regularly in the literary works of J.M. Synge, Eoin MacNeill, Máirtín Ó Direáin and Liam O'Flaherty (whose poem 'Na Blátha Craige' is reproduced opposite the title page).

The flora in pre-history

Pollen analysis of lake sediments shows the succession of plants growing in Ireland over the past tens of thousands of years. This includes evidence of plants from previous interglacial periods before the last Ice Age, such as Scots Pine and Rhododendron, which did not survive and which depended on man for their relatively recent reintroduction. An international study of the sediments in An Loch Mór on Inis Oírr (directed by Professor Michael O'Connell of NUI Galway) showed that in pre-history Aran was covered with woodland (oak, pine, elm, hazel, alder, birch, willow and then, later on, yew). Trunks of fir and oak were noted in the few surviving peat deposits on the islands in the early nineteenth century (O'Flaherty 1824).

Although the first farmers in Ireland date from the Neolithic Age (4000–2000 BC), the first real evidence of human habitation in Aran, provided by the wedge tombs in Inis Mór and Inis Meáin, is not until the Bronze Age (2000–600 BC). The Aran woodlands were gradually cleared by farmers from the Bronze Age onwards. Thus the present-day Aran environment, and its associated flora, is as much man-made as natural.

The flora – unique features

The most remarkable feature of the Aran/Burren flora is that it is a meeting-place of plants normally regarded as having Arctic–Alpine and Mediterranean–Atlantic affinities, all growing together near sea level. This unusual phenomenon has attracted international attention for centuries, with little consensus among botanists as to how it came about (Webb 1983). A warm period preceded the last Ice Age and may have allowed southern species to establish. Then the advancing glaciers may have brought seeds of northern origin. In any event, the present-day flora appears to have arisen mainly from the gradual and continuous migration of plants from Britain and continental Europe, together with some survivors from before the last Ice Age.

The flora – number of species

It is generally accepted that Ireland became an island about 7500 years ago, after the last Ice Age. The melting ice would have caused sea levels to rise by about 100 m, cutting off the land bridges to Great Britain, and also Aran from the Irish mainland. Due mainly to their relative isolation and less diverse habitats, islands usually have a smaller range of indigenous plant species (i.e. an 'impoverished' flora) compared to larger landmasses. Thus some 437 native species have been recorded in Aran (Webb 1980), compared to about 850 for the whole of Ireland, 1200 for Great Britain and 11,000 for all of Europe. Iceland is even more isolated than Ireland and has only about the same number of native species as Aran.

The flora – some oddities

Some 'exotic' plants (i.e. not native, or unexpected) are occasionally found in Aran. Gorse (Furze, Whin, *Ulex europaeus*), normally a calcifuge or lime-hating plant, is found growing in a few places on Inis Mór and around the football pitch at the Inis Meáin airstrip, the latter apparently introduced

3.2 Wych Elm grove, Inis Mór

with acidic soil shipped in from the mainland to lay out the pitch in 1988. Heathers[3.23] – also 'lime-haters' – occur regularly but are confined to patches of acidic soil such as boulder clay, and to the peaty sods in the solution hollows of the clints. In an otherwise practically treeless island, a grove of Wych Elms flourishes on Inis Mór[3.2] (see 'Trees' below).

Lucerne (Alfalfa, *Medicago sativa*) was introduced in the sandy coastal areas (machairs, see under 'Plants of seashore and sandy areas', below) in the late nineteenth century. This is a deep-rooted forage legume, used worldwide for grazing and haymaking. It continues to thrive when drought has restricted grass growth.[6.6] Sea-kale[3.58] (*Crambe maritima*) has been recorded recently on the foreshore on Inis Meáin and Inis Mór. It was first noted in the late seventeenth century (O'Flaherty 1684) and intermittently since then. Fuchsia[3.39] (*Fuchsia magellanica*), now well-established and often assumed to be native in Aran and throughout Connaught and west Munster, was introduced to Europe from southern Chile about 1790. Hops (*Humulus lupulus*) have been recorded intermittently at two monastic sites on Inis Mór, Teampall Bhreacáin and the former Franciscan monastery in Cill Éinne (founded in 1485 and demolished after the Reformation). It was still growing at the Cill Éinne site in 2005, where it may have been introduced for beer-brewing by medieval monks and has survived as a rare botanical relict.

In 1987, botanists were delighted to find Cornflower (*Centaurea cyanus*) and Darnel (*Lolium temulentum*) still growing on the islands (Curtis *et al.* 1988). These two species have been associated with tilled farmland since Biblical times, with Darnel mentioned as a weed of cereal crops in Matthew 13:24–30. They had been assumed to be extinct in Ireland since about 1970, due mainly to more effective seed cleaning and weed control, and to the decline in tillage. Both species are listed in *The Irish Red Data Book* (Curtis & McGough 1988).

As already mentioned, Purple Milk-vetch (*Astragalus danicus*) is found in Ireland only in Aran. The Aran flora also contains, as does the wider Irish flora, some Atlantic–Oceanic introductions from the Americas (e.g. Fuchsia from Chile) and from the southern hemisphere (e.g. Montbretia, *Crocosmia* x *crocosmiflora,* from southern Africa). As happens all along the west coast of Ireland, seeds of North American and Caribbean origin (e.g. Morning Glory, Sea-pea, Sea-bean, Horse-eye Bean and Nickar Nut) are regularly cast ashore. However, none of these are known to have germinated.

Folk medicine

Of the some 437 plant species recorded in Aran, medicinal uses have been claimed for more than 300 in the folklore of various countries. However, due to the general lack of clinical evaluation and to the difficulties in accurately identifying plants mentioned in folklore, any claims should be treated with caution. The same local name can be applied to a range of plants with widely different pharmacological properties. For example, *Méaracán Púca* can mean Harebell or Foxglove, and *glanrosc* can mean eyebright or Scarlet Pimpernel.

Many of the benefits claimed for medicinal herbs are rather general and non-specific, such as boosting the immune system, cleansing the blood or aiding digestion. If all the claimed medicinal benefits of the Aran flora were listed here it would read like a herbal or a health-store catalogue. Therefore, medicinal uses are mentioned only where such are fairly specific and generally recognized. Nowadays, the greater availability and acceptability in Aran of conventional medicine has led to a significant decline in folk remedies. Consequently, the islanders' knowledge of plants and their medicinal properties (ethnobotany) has also declined.

O'Flaherty (1824) noted that 'the islands abound with a variety of medicinal and sweet herbs'. Ó hEithir (1983) studied the traditional folk remedies used in the Aran Islands. These often employed combinations of a herb and an incantation (*artha*), the practitioners being known variously as *mná feasa*, *mná leighis* or *mná luibheanna* (wise, healing or herb women, respectively). The *mná luibheanna* were respected but also feared because of the belief that the first person they gazed on while picking herbs could get the disease of the patient for whom they were being gathered. Ó Síocháin (1962) lists a number of Aran seashore plants and seaweeds with medicinal properties. Medicinal plants in the Irish and wider European flora, many of which grow in Aran, are described in Irish by Williams (1993) and by Forey & Lindsay (1997).

Trees

Although folk memories of 'woods' (probably dense scrubland) in Aran have been recorded for the late 1700s and early 1800s, trees are now quite rare. This is due to the thin soil cover, the persistent high winds and the accompanying salt spray, which scorches young leaves. Such trees that occur are usually misshapen and wind-sculpted by the prevailing south-westerlies.[2.5] However, a few small groves of trees survive on Inis Mór, such as the stand of Wych Elm (*Ulmus glabra*) in a sheltered and fertile hollow in the grounds of the ruined St Thomas' church in Cill Rónáin.[3.2] These were planted in the late nineteenth century by the Church of Ireland rector, the Rev. William Kilbride. Although Dutch elm disease has eliminated most of the elms on the Irish mainland, the Aran specimens seem to have escaped, possibly because insect vectors carrying this fungal disease haven't yet managed to fly across Galway Bay.

Plant classification

Botanists use the Latin binomial system (genus followed by species, e.g. *Gentiana verna* for Spring Gentian) devised by the eighteenth-century Swedish scientist Linnaeus to name plants. It is the one accepted international system for classifying plants. It is rigorously logical, notwithstanding the inevitable confusion that arises from time to time when a familiar species gets renamed. At local level, however, a very wide and sometimes conflicting range of vernacular names, in both English and Irish, may be used for a particular plant. For example, in Britain and Ireland there are more than seventy local names for that most typical Aran flower, Bird's-foot Trefoil[3.51] (*Lotus corniculatus*).

Most of the publications on British and Irish flora attempt to standardize on single English or Irish names for each species. However, in listing the

Irish names of wild flowers in Aran the author frequently found the same name used for different plants, different names for the same plant, and some names that occur locally but are rare elsewhere (such as *Crúibíní* for the Stone Bramble,[3.8] *Rubus saxatilis*). In contrast to the extensive published literature of botanical and vernacular English plant names, the many Irish versions of such names have been largely confined to the oral tradition. Regrettably, many of these will disappear as farming becomes less important in Aran and if spoken Irish declines.

The Irish plant names used here are based both on official published lists, i.e. 'Census Catalogue of the Flora of Ireland' (Scannell & Synnott 1987) and *Ainmneacha Plandaí agus Ainmhithe* (Stationery Office 1978), and on the most common versions found in Aran. The English and botanical names, and the plant descriptions, are based largely on four key publications: *An Irish Flora* (Webb *et al.* 1996), *The Burren – a companion to the wildflowers of an Irish stone wilderness* (Nelson 1997), *Wild Plants of The Burren and the Aran Islands* (Nelson 1999), and *New Flora of the British Isles* (Stace 1997).

The Aran environment
The flora of the Aran Islands is determined by the local Burren-type environment, i.e.:

1. Limestone geology (high-calcium/high-pH soils), favouring calcicole (lime-loving) plants
2. Mild winters, strong winds limiting growth, proximity to the sea
3. High reflected light levels from rocks, sand and sea
4. Traditional farming in an unspoilt environment

Factors 1–3 will persist into the foreseeable future. However, farming will inevitably be influenced by changes in the wider agricultural economy and by environmental regulations. The current practice of winter grazing by livestock ensures not only reduced competition by grasses for Burren species in late spring/early summer but also limits scrub invasion of the pastures. The low-intensity farming system encourages species diversity and prevents grasses from shading and dominating the more sensitive Burren flora. These factors are discussed in greater detail in Chapter 6.

Plants of the limestone pavements and grykes

The limestone pavements and their fissures (grykes) comprise two quite distinct environments. The term 'pavement' in the Burren and Aran sense includes both the bare clints and where these have a thin cover of soil, whether natural or man-made. Such soils are dry and exposed, are grazed by livestock and suit species with Arctic–Alpine affinities. In contrast, the grykes are shaded, sheltered and dank, places where ferns of a more Mediterranean–Atlantic type thrive. Thus, plants of widely different geographical affinities are found growing happily together at sea level in Aran.

The natural soils are known as rendzinas (described in Chapter 6) and are derived from the weathering of limestone-based material. Although they have relatively low levels of the major plant nutrients potassium and phosphorus, they sustain a high nitrogen-fixing bacterial population. This encourages species diversity and prevents more aggressive and competitive grasses from dominating the sward.

Visitors to The Burren, particularly those in cars or buses, often express disappointment that all they see are vast stretches of bare rock rather than

3.3 Spring Gentian

the lush vegetation they may have been led to expect. Exotic plants do indeed occur, but they are adapted to survive the persistent strong winds and cool climate, and thus are either quite small and ground-hugging or take shelter deep in the grykes. They can only be observed properly by getting 'down-and-dirty' on one's knees.

Spring Gentian. *Gentiana verna. Bláth (Pabhsaer) Mhuire* [3.3]

The Spring Gentian is probably the most celebrated and attractive flower in The Burren and Aran, and is rightly regarded as the chief glory of the region. Its electric-blue flowers appear in April and May. It is named after King Gentius of Illyria, who ruled from 180–167 BC. Although found in the high Alps and arctic Russia and popularly regarded as an Arctic–Alpine, this designation is not strictly true since it is also found in the central plains of Germany and in the karst regions of Slovenia and Croatia. It is most visible where vegetation has been close-cropped by grazing, but is quite difficult to find when not in flower.

The Spring Gentian was first recorded in Ireland before 1650 by a Mr Heaton 'in the mountaines betwixt Gort and Galloway, abundantly' (How 1650). Although widespread in Aran, it is not nearly as common as in The Burren (Webb 1980). It also occurs around the shores of Lough Corrib, County Galway, and in south County Mayo; it is unknown elsewhere in Ireland, and in Britain is confined to a small area of the northern Pennines.

It is a densely tufted plant with single flowering stems about 50 mm high. The flowers are 5-petalled and solitary, intense blue, about 25 mm across, with small white scales between the petals. The leaves are about 10 mm long, oval and in a rosette pattern at soil level.

Bloody Crane's-bill. *Geranium sanguineum. Crobh Dearg* [3.4]

Bloody Crane's-bill is extremely abundant on the limestone pavements and pastures of Aran. In contrast to the more celebrated Spring Gentian (above) it blooms throughout the growing season. This, coupled with its abundance and attractiveness, would make it a prime candidate for consideration as the floral emblem of Aran.

Bloody Crane's-bill is a true geranium species, not be confused with the common household 'geranium' (*Pelargonium*). It grows particularly well in the local rendzina soils. Its name is usually assumed to derive from the reddish pointed seed pods that develop after flowering, but could also be from the

3.4 Bloody Crane's-bill; 3.5 Herb-Robert

scarlet colour of its older leaves. It is abundant in counties Clare and Galway but rare elsewhere. It was used in folk medicine as a specific against urinary disorders in both humans and animals.

The flowers are solitary, vivid purplish red (magenta), 5-petalled, 25–30 mm across. The leaves are circular in outline, deeply divided and turn scarlet before withering in the autumn.

Herb-Robert. *Geranium robertianum. Ruithéal Rí (Earball Rí)*[3.5]
Herb-Robert is a straggling hairy annual, common throughout Ireland on waste ground and roadsides and particularly abundant in Aran. Its odour

Clockwise from top right: **3.6** Irish Saxifrage; **3.7** Pyramidal Bugle; **3.8** Stone Bramble

apparently repels insects, hence one of its common names of Stinking Robert. It is a well-known medicinal herb for treating kidney diseases and to control bleeding. It has been used to treat 'red water' disease in cattle.

The flowers are reddish purple, 5-petalled, 12–20 mm across. The leaves are triangular in outline and have 5 deeply divided leaflets, which may be red-tinged in autumn.

SAXIFRAGES. *Saxifraga* spp.

The saxifrages (literally 'breaker of rocks' in Latin) are mainly Arctic–Alpine species with a world distribution in the Northern Hemisphere, but also extending down the Andes into South America. Two species, *S. rosacea* and *S. tridactylites*, have been recorded in Aran. London Pride is a saxifrage species (*S. urbium*) adapted for garden cultivation.

In Europe, the geographical range of saxifrages extends into the Arctic and the Alps, but they are rare in Ireland outside The Burren and Aran. Saxifrages are frequently associated with anthills, hence the local Irish name *Pabhsaer na Seangán* (Posy of the Ants).

Irish Saxifrage. *S. rosacea. Mórán Gaelach*[3.6]
Irish Saxifrage is a perennial, frequent and locally abundant on the lime-stone pavements and the roadsides of Aran, forming compact low-growing hummocks. It is also found in the south-west, the Galtee mountains, Iceland, the Faroes and, to a very limited extent, in central Europe. In Great Britain it was last recorded in Snowdonia about 1978.

The white flowers (sometimes tinged with pink), 12–20 mm across, on upright hairy stalks, bloom from April to July, and grow from compact rosettes of leaves. The leaf rosettes often turn bright red at flowering time.

Rue-leaved Saxifrage. *S. tridactylites. Mórán Balla*
Rue-leaved Saxifrage is a small annual, frequent on walls, roadsides and the limestone pavements. It blooms from late winter to spring.

The flowers are very small (petals 3 mm long) and white, with several on each erect, sticky stem. The rosette leaves have sticky glandular hairs and turn bright red in dry spells.

Pyramidal Bugle. *Ajuga pyramidalis. Glasair Bheannach*[3.7]
Although the Pyramidal Bugle is generally quite rare and is listed in *The Irish Red Data Book* (Curtis & McGough 1988), it is locally abundant on rocky ground in parts of Inis Mór. It is also found occasionally on Inis Meáin but not to date on Inis Oírr. It flowers for a short period in April and May but is otherwise quite inconspicuous. It was once considered to be unique to The Burren (including Aran) and western Connemara, but has since been found in Rathlin island (County Antrim), where it is a Scheduled Species. It was first recorded in 1854 as a native plant in Aran by David Moore (then Director of the Botanic Gardens).

Pyramidal Bugle is a dwarf, stumpy plant, with its small flowers almost concealed by the bracts. The stems are erect, 80–150 mm high, bearing pale bluish-violet flowers with 3-lobed lower lips. The tiered hairy bracts are usual-ly tinged bluish-purple and are longer than the small blue flowers. The leaves are dull green, hairy, oval, with the lower leaves tapering into a short stalk.

Stone Bramble. *Rubus saxatilis. Crúibíní (Sú na mBan Mín)*[3.8]
The Stone Bramble is very frequent on the limestone pavements. Its local name in Aran and in mainland County Galway is *Crúibíní* (little claws or hooves). Its 'official' name in Irish, and as used in County Clare when it was

45

Irish-speaking, is *Sú na mBan Mín*, which intriguingly means 'The (red) berry of the gentle women'. Traditionally, it was gathered in Aran on St Mac Dara's Day, 16 July. Like many fruits, it contains vitamin C and has been used to prevent scurvy.

As a *Rubus* species, Stone Bramble is related to the Blackberry (*R. fruticosus*) and the Raspberry (*R. idaeus*), but in Ireland is confined largely to the Burren/Aran region. Although often believed to be unique to this region, it is also found on calcareous (lime-rich) soils in Greenland, Iceland, Russia, the Himalayas and Japan.

The leaves are 30–80 mm long, in appearance like strawberry leaves, with toothed margins and hairy underneath. The plants bear off-white 8 mm flowers in June and July. These mature into clusters of 2–6 ruby-red fruits (drupes), which are flavoursome but somewhat tart.

Harebell (Scotch Bluebell). *Campanula rotundifolia. Méaracán Gorm* [3.9]

The Harebell is locally frequent or abundant in Aran and The Burren. There are numerous Irish versions of its name, usually based on *méaracán* (thimble), e.g. *Méaracán Gorm* (blue thimble), *Méaracán Táilliúra* (tailor's thimble) and *Méaracán Púca* (goblin's thimble). In folklore, it is regarded as protected by the 'Little People' (hence *Méaracán Púca*).

The Harebell is one of the most striking and beautiful of the Aran flowers and can be seen regularly on the road verges and the limestone pavements from mid-summer to autumn. The lowermost leaves are heart-shaped or round. The flowers are sky-blue in colour (occasionally pinkish-blue to white), bell-shaped (hence *Campanula*), drooping, 5-lobed, up to 20 mm long and usually solitary.

Irish Eyebright. *Euphrasia salisburgensis. Róisnín Radhairc (Glanrosc Gaelach)* [3.10]

Eyebright (*Euphrasia*) is a member of the snapdragon family (Scrophulariaceae) and up to a dozen species of this genus have been recorded in the Irish flora. The various species are difficult to tell apart and hybridization creates further confusion. The eyebrights are facultative parasites (hemiparasites), i.e. not true parasites, on other plant species such as thyme. However, they have green leaves and can produce some of their own nutrients.

The common names of *Euphrasia* in English, in some other European languages and in Irish (*Róisnín Radhairc, Glanrosc Gaelach* and *Lus na Súl*),

3.9 Harebell; 3.10 Irish Eyebright

3.11 Primrose; 3.12 Cowslip

often refer to the eye or eyesight. It is not surprising, therefore, that it is commonly recommended in folk medicine as a cure for eye disorders.

One of the commonest eyebright species in Aran is *Euphrasia salisburgensis*. It blooms from July to September on the limestone pavements and is often associated with thyme, on which it is a hemiparasite.

It is a bushy little plant with bronze-tinged leaves and stems. It is also locally frequent on lime-rich soils in western counties (Limerick to Donegal) but unknown in the east of Ireland. It does not occur in Great Britain and its nearest location south of Ireland is in the Vosges region of France.

It is easily identified and does not hybridize. The leaves are oval, jagged-toothed with the bronze stems bearing quite small (about 5 mm) yellow-eyed white flowers. The seed capsules are hairless.

Primrose. *Primula vulgaris. Sabhaircín* 3.11

The Primrose is well-known throughout Ireland and Britain and is usually found in semi-shaded field boundaries. However, this plant is often abundant in more exposed habitats in Aran, as the greater cloud cover of the west of Ireland provides partial shade. It can flower from as early as Christmas

(Primrose is from the Latin *prima rosa*, first rose of the year) and its appearance is welcomed as a sign that winter is nearly over. It is a close relative of the Cowslip (see below).

The leaves are greyish-green, in rosettes, and tapered at the base. The sulphur-yellow, solitary, 25–35 mm flowers on long hairy stems are abundant in April and May and easily identifiable. *Pabhsaer Naomh Iosef* (St Joseph's Posy) is one of its local names in Aran, but this may also refer to the Cowslip.

In folk medicine, the Primrose was well-known for treating various nervous conditions. It also has some culinary uses. It was used to prevent the fairies spoiling butter and milk and on the first of May would be scattered on the threshold or tied to the tails of livestock to ward off evil spirits.

Cowslip. *Primula veris. Bainne Bó Bleachtáin* [3.12]

The Cowslip is a calcicole (lime-loving) plant and is the second common *Primula* species in Aran. Its name, due to its association with grazing pastures, is a polite version of the Old English 'cu-sloppe' (cow slop). It is becoming increasingly rare throughout Ireland and is a Scheduled Species in Northern Ireland. It cannot compete with the vigorous well-fertilized ryegrass swards of modern farming and, in addition, silage-cutting in May and June limits seed set.

The leaves are somewhat similar to those of the Primrose (above), but are more paddle-shaped and the leaf-stalks are as long as the blades. It blooms in April and May, with small (10–15 mm across), deep yellow, cup-shaped flowers, in drooping clusters on erect hairy stems. In Aran, the Cowslip and the Primrose frequently hybridize (False Oxlip, *Primula x tommasinii*), with the resulting flowers being somewhat between the two in appearance. One of its local names is *Pabhsaer Naomh Iosef* (which may also refer to the Primrose, above) and its official Irish name, *Bainne Bó Bleachtáin*, can also mean dandelion. Like Primrose, the Cowslip is reputed to have various medicinal and culinary uses.

Purple Milk-vetch. *Astragalus danicus. Bleachtphiseán* [3.13]

Purple Milk-vetch is remarkable in that it is found only on Inis Mór (north-west of Dún Aonghasa [1.2] and near Port Daibhche) and Inis Meáin (near Trá Leitreach and Trá Mhaindlín) and nowhere else in Ireland. It was first noted in Aran in the early nineteenth century. It is one of almost 90

Protected Species in the Irish Republic under various Flora Protection Orders and is listed in *The Irish Red Data Book* (Curtis & McGough 1988). Seeds of this plant are deep-frozen in the Irish Threatened Plant Genebank. The Genebank is maintained by Trinity College Dublin as a reserve of species that might become extinct. There is no convincing explanation as to why it grows in Aran but nowhere else in Ireland; it may have lingered as a relict from an inter-glacial warm period. It is predominantly a continental European species but is also common in eastern England.

The plant is a perennial legume, growing in rocky areas and stabilized sand dunes, with prostrate or straggling stems up to 35 cm long. The leaves consist of 6–12 oval leaflets arranged in pairs on opposite sides of the midrib. The flowers are usually purple, each 15–18 mm long, and appear from spring to early summer, in compact clover-like heads. The fruits are ovoid, hairy and flattened.

As a Protected Species, there are many restrictions on the use of sites where this plant grows. In particular, such sites may not be cultivated, developed or built on. As part of the EU Rural Environment Protection Scheme (REPS), the agricultural advisory service (Teagasc) shows Aran farmers how to identify this rare species.[6.8]

3.13 Purple Milk-vetch; 3.14 Tufted Vetch

3.15 Wild Thyme

Tufted (Common) Vetch. *Vicia cracca. Peasair na Luch* 3.14
Tufted Vetch is a scrambling perennial legume, common throughout Ireland, and found occasionally along the roadsides and walls of Aran. Its masses of bluish-purple flowers are conspicuous from June to August.

The leaves are tendril-tipped and are divided into 12–30 leaflets, each 10–25 mm long. The flowers are about 10 mm long, pea-like, with up to 40 flowers in each elongated (up to 10 cm) dense spike.

Wild Thyme. *Thymus praecox. Tím Chreige* 3.15
Wild Thyme is abundant throughout Aran, especially on the limestone pavements and rocky ledges. The leaves are aromatic, particularly when crushed. It is frequently parasitized by Dodder, eyebrights and Broomrape. In folk medicine it has been used to treat nervous conditions and other ailments.

The leaves are small (less than 10 mm), dark green and ground-hugging. The flowers are small, pale purple and clustered in rounded heads.

Wild Strawberry. *Fragaria vesca. Sú Talún Fiáin* 3.16
Wild Strawberry is frequent on the limestone pavements and roadsides of Aran, growing as a low perennial with long rooting runners. The fruits are

Clockwise from top left: **3.16** Wild Strawberry; **3.17** Lady's Bedstraw; **3.18** Meadowsweet; **3.19** Hemp-agrimony

quite tasty, though much smaller than commercial varieties, and are rich in vitamin C. The leaves have many applications in folk medicine.

The leaves are bright green, with 3 oval leaflets, each about 50 mm long. The flowers are 5-petalled, 15–20 mm across, white and borne on branched erect stems.

Lady's Bedstraw. *Galium verum. Boladh Cnis (Rú Mhuire)*[3.17]

The fluffy yellow flowers of Lady's Bedstraw are very noticeable and abundant in Aran pastures in mid-summer. Apart from its visual appeal it has many reputed medicinal uses, such as in stopping external bleeding. In the home it has been used for curdling milk and as a pleasant-smelling bedding material (hence its Irish name *Boladh Cnis*).

The leaves are fine and needle-shaped, 8–20 mm long, in whorls of 8–12 around the 4-angled stems. The bright yellow flowers are very small (2–4 mm across), 4-petalled, in dense clusters.

Meadowsweet. *Filipendula ulmaria. Airgead Luachra*[3.18]

Meadowsweet is a prominent herb (30–70 cm), with hairy stems, locally frequent in damp ground in Aran. Its English name derives from its sweet smell. It is well recognized as a medicinal herb for various ailments, possibly because it contains salicylic acid (the active ingredient of aspirin). The religious leaders of pre-Christian Ireland (the Druids) included meadowsweet in their list of 'most-sacred' plants.

The leaves are dark green, but white on the lower surface, with 3–5 pairs of leaflets. The flowers are creamy-white, usually 5-petalled, each 3–6 mm across.

Hemp-agrimony. *Eupatorium cannabinum. Cnáib Uisce* (Scothóg Mhuire) [3.19]

Hemp-agrimony is very frequent in Aran, growing mainly out of the limestone grykes. In contrast to its erect growth habit on the mainland, in Aran it is dwarfed by the persistent high winds. Hart (1875) commented that 'droll little specimens of *Eupatorium cannabinum*, a couple of inches high, are constantly arresting the attention'. Its official Irish name of *Cnáib Uisce* derives from its association with wet areas on the mainland.

The leaves are opposite, stalked, green, with 3–5 toothed leaflets 5–10 cm long. It blooms in late summer, with very small pale pink flowers, in fluffy clusters.

3.20 Purple-loosestrife

3.21 Ox-eye Daisy; 3.22 Scarlet Pimpernel

Purple-loosestrife. *Lythrum salicaria. Créachtach (Earball Caitín)*[3.20]
Purple-loosestrife is common in damp places throughout Ireland and in Aran is noticeable around marshes and growing out of the grykes.

The leaves are opposite, 5–10 cm long, dark green, willow-like, on tall (up to 1.5 m) upright stems. The flowers are 4–6-petalled, in dense, deep-magenta whorls, about 15 mm across, in terminal spikes.

Ox-eye Daisy. *Leucanthemum vulgare. Nóinín Mór*[3.21]
The Ox-eye Daisy is common throughout Ireland and is particularly abundant in Aran on roadsides and waste ground. In folk medicine it was used to treat coughs and a wide range of other ailments.

The leaves are dark green, toothed, in rosettes at ground level. The flowers are typical of daisies but much larger (as the Irish name *Nóinín Mór* implies), up to 50 mm across, on upright stems.

Scarlet Pimpernel. *Anagallis arvensis. Falcaire Fiáin*[3.22]
The Scarlet Pimpernel is a hairless annual, common throughout Ireland and abundant in Aran on roadsides and waste ground. It is a medicinal herb in many countries, used as a cure for gripe in infants, falling sickness, madness, toothache and eye disorders (hence known as *Glanrosc,* 'clear vision', in parts of County Cork).

The leaves are opposite, stalkless, oval or ovate-lanceolate, 5–15 mm

3.23 Common Heather; 3.24 Squinancywort

long. The flowers are red, 5-lobed, 4–8 mm, on slender stalks. The flower heads close by mid-afternoon and in humid weather.

Common (Ling) Heather. *Calluna vulgaris. Fraoch Mór*[3.23]
Common or Ling Heather is a woody plant, widespread on acid peat throughout Ireland. Although a calcifuge (lime-hating) species it is also, and unexpectedly, common on the limestone pavements of Aran. However, it is mainly restricted to peaty (acidic) hummocks in the solution hollows of the limestone, or to patches of boulder clay. Over time, rain has leached out lime from the hummocks and the carbonic acid in the rain also helps to maintain acidity.

The leaves are dark green, very small and scale-like (3 mm), crowded and overlapping along the stems. The flowers are mauve or pink (sometimes white), very small (4–5 mm long) and clustered in long, dense spikes, with a pleasant aroma. Heather has many applications in folk medicine.

Bell Heather (Heath). *Erica cinerea. Fraoch Cloigíneach*
Bell Heather is found in similar habitats as Common Heather (above) in Aran. It is usually rarer than Common Heather, possibly because it is less tolerant of limestone-derived soils.

The dark-green leaves are very small, needle-like, in whorls along the stems, about 5 mm long. The purple-red flowers are very small (5–6 mm), in erect spikes, and are distinctly bell or urn shaped.

55

Clockwise from top left: 3.25 Yellow-rattle; 3.26 Wild Leek; 3.27 Common Mallow

Squinancywort. *Asperula cynanchica. Lus na hAincise*[3.24]

Squinancywort is a prostrate perennial, frequent on the Aran pavements and sand dunes but very rare outside the south-west (Kerry to Galway).

The leaves are bright green, fine and needle-shaped, 5–20 mm long, mostly in whorls of 4. The flowers are very small (2–4 mm across), white or pale pink, 4-petalled, scented, in clusters at the tips of the stems.

Yellow-rattle. *Rhinanthus minor. Gliográn*[3.25]

Yellow-rattle is a hemiparasitic annual, 10–30 cm tall, common throughout Ireland but particularly frequent in Aran pastures. In late summer the flower capsules contain black seeds that rattle as you brush past, hence the common name for this plant.

The leaves are opposite, oblong, green, with toothed margins. The flowers are yellow, tubular, up to 15 mm long with 2 lips, the lower 3-lobed.

Wild Leek. *Allium ampeloprasum* var. *babingtonii*. *Cainneann*[3.26]

Wild Leek is a real curiosity, usually found in Ireland only around the west and north-west coasts. It is an unmistakable member of the Aran flora, frequent along walls and roadsides. It has various other common names in English and Irish, such as Babington's Leek, Wild Garlic, *Gairleog Fiáin* and *Oinniún Fiáin*. Its origins are disputed but it is an Atlantic species, with Ireland as its most northerly location. It is probably very ancient and may have been introduced by early man in Ireland, which was later dispersed from gardens and became naturalized.

Although Wild Leek is still used occasionally in Aran as a culinary herb it is best known for its medicinal properties. It has been used to reduce bleeding from cuts and for various respiratory ailments. It was formerly grown in small quantities in garden plots as an anthelminthic for treating parasitic worms (Colgan 1893). Like other members of the onion family, it will taint milk and butter if eaten by cows (Lewis 1837).

The leaves are grey-green, long and grass-like, 10–30 mm wide, tending to flop and wither at flowering time. They are frequently infected with a rust fungus (*Uromyces ambiguus*), appearing as small orange pustules on the leaves. The flowers are on tall (1–2 m) slender stalks, globular, with 6 pale-purple petals.

Common Mallow. *Malva sylvestris*. *Lus na Meall Mhuire*[3.27]

Common Mallow is a straggling or nearly erect (up to 60 cm) perennial herb, frequent along roadsides and waste ground in Aran. The flowers are numerous, pink with purple veins, with 5 well-separated petals, each about 15 mm wide. In folk medicine it has been used to treat cuts and sprains.

Common Mallow can be confused with another Aran mallow – Tree Mallow (*Lavatera arborea*, *Hocas Ard*). However, Tree Mallow is more erect, shrub-like and taller (up to 1 m), and has flowers varying in colour from lilac to purple, with deep-purple veins and base. It is regarded as a 'garden escape', most usually found near houses.

Devil's-bit Scabious. *Succisa pratensis*. *Odhrach Bhallach*[3.28]

Devil's-bit Scabious is common in damp grasslands throughout Ireland

Clockwise from left: **3.28** Devil's-bit Scabious; **3.29** Hoary Rock-rose; **3.30** Early-purple Orchid

and is noticeable in the Aran limestone pavements and pastures in late summer. The name derives from the truncated ('bitten-off') appearance of the tap root.

The leaves are hairy, oval to spoon-shaped, forming a rosette at ground level. The flowers are small, blue-purple, clustered in globular heads 30–35 mm across and borne on stalks up to 50 cm high.

Hoary Rock-rose. *Helianthemum oelandicum. Grianrós Liath* [3.29]
The Hoary Rock-rose, a plant with southern affinities, is listed in *The Irish Red Data Book* (Curtis & McGough 1988) as 'Rare' and is confined mainly

to County Clare and to the Aran Islands. It is widespread, though local, only on the limestone pavements of Inis Mór. It is a wild relative of the garden rock-roses but unrelated to conventional roses (genus *Rosa*). It was first recorded in Aran by Andrews (1845).

The leaves are opposite, 5–8 mm long, slightly glossy dark green with silvery felt underneath, on wiry stems. The 5-petalled pale-yellow flowers, up to 10 mm across, appear in May soon after the Spring Gentian.

ORCHIDS

Twenty-three of Ireland's twenty-seven wild orchids grow in Aran and The Burren. These rare and exotic plants require a special root relationship with various fungi in order to flower. Orchid derives from the Greek *orkhis* for testicle, based on the appearance of its (often paired) underground tubers. The Irish name for orchid, *magairlín*, is the diminutive of testicle. Not surprisingly, in folklore various orchid species have been recommended as aphrodisiacs. Many other medicinal and culinary uses have also been claimed for orchids.

Early-purple Orchid. *Orchis mascula*. Magairlín Meidhreach (Pabhsaer Bealtaine) [3.30]

The Early-purple Orchid is one of the commonest orchids found in Aran pastures and field edges, flowering mainly in April and May. Its supposed aphrodisiac effect is recognized in its Irish name, *Magairlín Meidhreach*. *Magairlín* means orchid and *meidhreach* usually translates as 'merry' but in this case means 'wanton' or 'lustful'. Brian Merriman includes it, along with other herbal love potions, in his eighteenth-century poem 'Cúirt an Mheon-Oíche' (The Midnight Court):

> *Greamanna dh'úlla is púdar luibheanna,*
> *Magairlín meidhreach, …*
> (Apple pieces and powdered herbs,
> The wanton orchid, …)

The stems are 12–35 cm high, bearing rosettes of 4–8 oblong, glossy, blue-tipped leaves at ground level, often with dark purple-black spots. The flowers, borne in cylindrical spikes (about 20 flowers per spike), are reddish-purple to white, 20 mm across, with 3-lobed lips.

3.31 Pyramidal Orchid

Pyramidal Orchid. *Anacamptis pyramidalis. Magairlín na Stuaice*[3.31]
The Pyramidal Orchid is common throughout Ireland on lime-rich soils and is particularly noticeable in Aran in mid-summer.

There are 3–4 grey-green leaves around the base and about 5 smaller ones on the stem. The dark magenta flowering spike tapers distinctly towards the tip.

Common Spotted-orchid. *Dactylorhiza fuchsii. Nuacht Bhallach*[3.32]
Spotted orchids (*Dactylorhiza* spp.) are 'occasional' in Aran. They comprise a very confusing group; it is difficult to distinguish between the various species and there have been numerous name changes.

The Common Spotted-orchid (*D. fuchsii*) can be distinguished from other Aran orchids mainly by its mauve or pink flowers. These have flat, broad lips with the centre lobe prominent, triangular, equal to or longer than the two side lobes. The leaves, usually less than 7, have brownish-purple spots.

Dense-flowered Orchid (Irish Orchid). *Neotinea maculata.*
Magairlín Glas[3.33]
The Dense-flowered Orchid is a Mediterranean–Atlantic species found in Europe, North Africa and Asia Minor, and also in Madeira and the Canary

3.32 Common Spotted-orchid; 3.33 Dense-flowered Orchid

Islands. Ireland is its most northerly location in Europe, hence its alternative name of Irish Orchid. In Britain it has been found only in the Isle of Man, where it was last recorded in 1986 and is now believed extinct.

This orchid is a Burren (including Aran) speciality. It is infrequent and its pale-green flowers make it difficult to find. It blooms early, about the same time as the Spring Gentian, giving the scientifically intriguing combination of an Arctic–Alpine and a Mediterranean–Atlantic plant appearing together.

The leaves are pale green, with 2–3 larger leaves at the base and smaller leaves on the flowering stems. The stems are 12–25 cm long, bearing pale greenish-cream spikes. The flowers are 3–4 mm across, pale green, never opening very fully.

Bee Orchid. *Ophrys apifera. Magairlín na mBeach* 3.34
The distinctive and striking Bee Orchid has been recorded as 'occasional' in Inis Mór and Inis Meáin, and was found once by the author on Inis Oírr. Ireland is its most northerly location in Europe and it is a Scheduled Species in Northern Ireland. Its bee-like flowers make it one of the most identifiable plants in Aran. The peculiar flowers are assumed to have originally evolved to attract pollinating bees, but they are now usually self-pollinated in Ireland.

The Bee Orchid is a strictly calcicole (lime-loving) species, often found colonizing bare sandy areas before more vigorous and competitive plants take over. It flowers in June and July, bearing 3–6 blooms, each about 12 mm across, on each spike. The leaves are green in winter and wither when the flowers develop.

Shrubs and bushes

Honeysuckle (Woodbine, Irish Ivy). *Lonicera periclymenum.*
Féithleann (Bainne Gabhan) 3.35
Honeysuckle is very abundant on the Aran pavements and walls, and in the grykes. It has a pleasant scent when the buds open in the evenings, allowing pollination by hawkmoths and hover flies. As its alternative English name of 'Woodbine' suggests, this shrub is usually associated with semi-shade throughout Europe. However, in Aran and The Burren it is regularly found

3.34 Bee Orchid; 3.35 Honeysuckle

63

in the open, possibly due to the lower incidence there of bright sunshine. In folk medicine it has been used to treat eye disorders, fungal infections and fevers.

The leaves are opposite, grey-green, oval, about 50 mm long. The trumpet-shaped flowers are in clusters, creamy-yellow and tinged with red or purple. It bears round, red to purple-brown berries after flowering.

Hawthorn (Whitethorn). *Crataegus monogyna. Sceach Geal*[3.36]
The well-known Hawthorn is 'occasional' throughout Aran. Its growth is stunted by the high winds and salt spray[2.5] and it can only thrive in the lee of the stone walls.

Much folklore and superstition is associated with the Hawthorn and its supposed magical powers are a sometimes contradictory mixture of pagan and Christian beliefs. One of its common names, 'May-bush', is associated with the Celtic festival of *Bealtaine* (May), when it is in flower and when it is claimed to protect cattle and crops from the fairies. Where it grows near holy wells it is often decorated with coloured rags in May. Given Hawthorn's prominence in folklore, it is not surprising that many medicinal and culinary uses have been attributed to it.

The dull-green leaves are somewhat triangular, deeply lobed, and borne

3.36 Hawthorn

3.37 Blackthorn; 3.38 Hazel

on spiny branches. The flowers are 12 mm across, 5-petalled, white or pink, appearing after the leaves (in contrast to Blackthorn, below). The fruits are numerous, red and berry-like.

Blackthorn. *Prunus spinosa. Draighean*[3.37]

Blackthorn is one of the commonest shrubs in Aran. It is frequent on the limestone pavements, though usually quite stunted by the wind and salt spray.

The leaves are alternate, oval, finely toothed, 20–35 mm long, on dark spiny stems. Its flowers appear from March onwards, before the leaves (in contrast to Hawthorn, above), and are white, 5-petalled, 10–15 mm across. The fruits (sloes) are 12 mm across, distinctly bluish-black in colour with a waxy bloom. They have a very astringent taste and have been used to flavour gin. The plant also has numerous applications in folk medicine.

Hazel. *Corylus avellana. Coll*[3.38]

If farming were abandoned, Hazel would become the climax vegetation of Aran and The Burren. It is frequent in sheltered and inaccessible places on Inis Mór and Inis Meáin, but appears to be extinct on Inis Oírr. Hazel was afforded special protection in the eighth-century Irish tract *Bretha Comaithchesa*, which listed it as one of the 'nobles of the wood' (Nelson & Walsh 1993).

The leaves are alternate, shortly stalked, round or broadly oval, roughly hairy on both sides, toothed, 6–10 cm across. The familiar fruit is a nut, 15 mm long, surrounded by ragged leafy bracts.

Fuchsia. *Fuchsia magellanica. Fiúise*[3.39]

The spectacular Fuchsia hedges of western Ireland are a delight to visitors and locals alike. The shrub is common on Inis Mór and Inis Meáin, but apparently absent from Inis Oírr. It has various local names in Irish, such as *Deora Dé, Milíní* and *Mileanna Dearga*.

Fuchsia originated in south Chile and was introduced to Europe about 1790. Although now regarded as naturalized in Ireland, this is not strictly true as it is usually sterile and therefore does not set seed. Only on Inis Meáin is there clear evidence of it being spread by seed (Webb 1980).

Two 'races' of Fuchsia grow in Ireland and in Aran: 1) the original *F. magellanica*, with 4 dusky red sepals and slender elongated buds, and 2) var. *riccartonii*, introduced in Scotland in the mid-nineteenth century. This has scarlet-red sepals, fat buds, the lower bulbous and can be 'popped' when squeezed.

Juniper. *Juniperus communis. Aiteal*[3.40]

Juniper was one of the first shrubs to recolonize Ireland in the early postglacial period about 12,000 years ago. It is frequent in a few places on Inis Mór and Inis Meáin. Due to wind exposure it has a more prostrate habit in Aran than on the mainland.

3.39 Fuchsia; 3.40 Juniper

3.41 Burnet Rose

Branches of Yew (*Taxus baccata*) are used on the Irish mainland to represent palm fronds in Palm Sunday religious ceremonies. Since Yew is absent in Aran, Juniper has been adopted as the local substitute for palms. At one stage, the single known Juniper on Inis Oírr was in danger of being snipped to extinction. Although a second specimen had been discovered by the botanist Nathaniel Colgan (1893), by 1980 this species had apparently become extinct on Inis Oírr (Webb 1980).

The leaves are needle-shaped and sharp, dark bluish-green, about 10 mm long, bearing pale bluish-green cones. The plants can be either male or female, with the latter producing oily blue-black berries. The plant has numerous applications in folk medicine and the berries are used for flavouring gin.

Burnet Rose (Scotch Rose). *Rosa pimpinellifolia. Briúlán (Rós Fiáin)*[3.41]

Burnet Rose is an erect shrub (up to 50 cm tall). It is the most abundant wild rose species found in Aran, typically growing on the 'shattered' type

3.42 Elder

of limestone pavement. Even when out of bloom, it can be readily identified by its numerous very sharp spines. The mature rose hips are rich in vitamin C and have been used to treat scurvy and other ailments.

The leaves are small, green, with toothed margins and each with 7–11 oval leaflets. The flowers are solitary, 5-petalled, up to 40 mm across, white to creamy-pink. The rose hips (fruits) are purplish-black, occasionally red, with a persistent ring of black sepals.

Willow. *Salix* spp. *Saileach*
A number of willow species grow in moist areas at the foot of the limestone terraces in Aran. Their identification can be difficult, particularly since many hybrids occur. *Salix viminalis* (Osier) is one of the commonest species and was traditionally used to make various household items and baskets for carrying seaweed and turf (peat). Examples of such baskets can be seen in the island museums. Aran willows were noted for their quality and length and were often bartered for turf from Connemara.

Willows have many applications in folk medicine, particularly for pain and fever relief. The plant contains salicylic acid (named from *Salix*), the active ingredient of aspirin.

Elder. *Sambucus nigra. Trom*[3.42]

The Elder is found in Aran, either self-sown or planted, in the lee of walls or on the clay layers under the limestone terraces. It has a formidable presence in mythology and folk medicine. It was reputed to be the tree from which Judas hanged himself, and from which the cross of Christ was made. Its sinister reputation restricted its uses, e.g. it would not be used for firing or for making boats; it was thought a baby would not thrive in a cradle made from it and that a boy or animal would cease to grow if struck with it.

Elder was used to treat various human and animal ailments, including sprains, and as an infusion to induce sweating in colds. The leaves have insecticidal properties.

Elder is a small deciduous tree with grey corky bark and pithy stems. The leaves are 5–15 cm long, with 5–9 oval leaflets. The flowers are in creamy-white flat-topped masses (cymes), maturing into the familiar dark-purple fruits (elderberries). The berries are used for flavouring and colouring various foods and drinks.

Parasitic plants

Dodder. *Cuscuta epithymum. Clamhán*[3.43]

Although relatively rare and confined to some coastal areas of Ireland, the parasitic plant Dodder is common on stabilized dune grasslands in Inis

3.43 Dodder

3.44 Ivy Broomrape

Mór and Inis Meáin. It was possibly introduced in Aran as it was not recorded before 1892 (Nowers & Wells 1892). Doyle (1993) recorded it in The Burren as parasitic on nearly fifty host species but most commonly on thyme, Bird's-foot Trefoil, Squinancywort, Lady's Bedstraw, Red Clover, Yarrow and violets.

Dodder can best be described as looking like a jumbled heap of pink or yellow wires. The plant lacks chlorophyll and roots, and the leaves are reduced to minute scales.

Broomrape. *Orobanche* spp. *Múchóg* [3.44]
Two species of *Orobanche*, *O. hederae* and *O. minor*, are widespread in Aran. The former is a parasite only of ivy whereas the latter has a wide host range. Ireland is the most northerly location in Europe of *O. hederae* and it is a Scheduled Species in Northern Ireland.

The stems are erect, 12–60 cm tall. The flowering spikes and leaves have a distinctive brown papery appearance when mature.

Ferns (pteridophytes)

Maidenhair Fern. *Adiantum capillus-veneris. Dúchosach (Tae Scailpeach)* [3.45]
Maidenhair Fern is well-known and popular as a house plant. Its natural distribution includes the tropics, the Mediterranean, the Azores and Madeira. It is a delicate plant, sensitive to frost and wind, and in Ireland is rare outside Aran and The Burren. It is locally abundant in Aran and was noted there in 'great plenty' by Lhwyd on his Irish tour of 1700 (Lhwyd 1712). That was the first 'official' record (i.e. by a botanist) of a plant species for an Irish offshore island.

Maidenhair Fern has many uses in folk medicine. In Aran, the Irish name *Tae Scailpeach* (Tea of the Grykes) implies a herbal tea. Decoctions of the plant were regularly used for colds and lung complaints, to the extent that visiting botanists complained that there were fewer specimens left for them to find (Ogilby 1845). Nowers & Wells (1892) noted that improved ferry services made the plant 'subject to the depredations of Sunday trippers from Galway'. Nowadays, more than 200,000 tourists visit Aran each year, posing an even greater threat to the plant's survival.

Maidenhair Fern is a tender plant, finding shade and moisture in the grykes as well as protection from frost, wind and salt spray. It is also found along moist horizontal cracks on cliff faces.

The fronds are pale green, distinctly fan- or diamond-shaped, about 1 cm long, on glossy brownish-black stalks (hence the Irish name *Dúchosach*). The undersides of the leaves are covered with numerous dark brown reproductive structures (sori). A parasitic rust fungus, *Hyalospora adianti-capilli-veneris*, has been found infecting this fern in Inis Mór (Webb & Scannell 1983).

Hart's-tongue Fern. *Phyllitis scolopendrium. Creamh na Muice Fia (Teanga Chapaill)* [3.46]

Hart's-tongue Fern is common in Irish woodlands, particularly in limestone areas. In Aran it is found abundantly in the grykes and has been used to treat burns and chapped lips.

The strap-like fronds, 20–70 cm long, are bright green when young but later may become rather weather-beaten. Chlorosis (yellowing) of the leaves is common in Aran, due to the inherently low iron content of the soils. The undersides of the fronds show parallel bands of brown reproductive structures (sporangia).

Wall-rue. *Asplenium ruta-muraria. Luibh na Seacht nGábh* [3.47]

Wall-rue is common throughout Ireland, particularly on mortared walls. In Aran it is frequent on the drystone walls and particularly in the grykes. Its Irish name translates intriguingly as 'the herb of the seven perils'.

It is a small, unmistakable fern with thick, leathery dark-green fronds with diamond- or oval-shaped tips. The reproductive structures (sori), about 2 mm across, merge to cover most of the undersides of the fronds.

Maidenhair Spleenwort. *Asplenium trichomanes. Lus na Seilge* [3.48]

Maidenhair Spleenwort is common throughout Ireland, particularly on mortared walls. It is abundant on the limestone pavements and walls of Aran.

The slender fronds are strap-shaped, 5–20 cm, bright grass-green when young but darker when old, on black stalks. The lobes are oval and pointed at the tip. Reproductive structures (sori) occur on the undersides of the fronds and are about 2 mm long.

Rusty-back Fern. *Ceterach officinarum. Raithneach Rua* [3.49]

The Rusty-back Fern is plentiful in limestone areas of Ireland. It is common

Clockwise from top left: **3.45** Maidenhair Fern; **3.46** Hart's-tongue Fern; **3.47** Wall-rue; **3.48** Maidenhair Spleenwort

in Aran, where it grows particularly well (fronds up to 40 cm long, compared with the normal 10 cm). It is a hardy plant, surviving sodden winters and scorching summers. Its name derives from the appearance of the shrivelled-up backs of the fronds in dry periods.

The fronds are dark green, pinnately divided into rounded lobes, thickly covered with scales on the back.

3.49 Rusty-back Fern; 3.50 Polypody Fern

Polypody Fern. *Polypodium australe. Scim Leathan* [3.50]
Polypody Fern is very frequent on the limestone pavements and walls in Aran, though often stunted and wind-shrivelled.

The fronds are broadly triangular, bright green, divided into many strap-like lobes with rounded tips. In sheltered locations the leaves can grow up to 25 cm long. Round orange reproductive structures (sori) develop on the backs of the lobes in late summer.

Plants of seashore and sandy areas

The seashore and the sand dunes of Aran are home to a number of interesting plants. Such plants have to be adapted to the demanding conditions of low fertility, wind exposure, salt spray and drought. Thus they may be deep-rooted to survive winds and drought (e.g. Marram[3.62] and Sea Beet[3.61]), or have short life cycles so that seed-set is completed before summer droughts (e.g. Bird's-foot Trefoil[3.51]).

A stable, level, grassy coastal area on wind-blown calcareous sand is defined botanically as a machair (from the Scots Gaelic/Irish *machaire*, a low-lying fertile plain). They are common along the exposed west coasts of Ireland and Scotland (Bassett & Curtis 1985). They have a high seashell content (up to 80 or 90 per cent) and are species-rich. Machairs in Ireland are associated with placenames containing the words 'maghera' (from *machaire*) and 'muirbheach' along the Donegal and Galway coasts, respectively. They are often developed as sports pitches or golf links. In Aran, machairs are confined mainly to areas around Cill Mhuirbhigh and Cill Éinne on Inis Mór, and near the airstrips on Inis Meáin and Inis Oírr.

Bird's-foot Trefoil. *Lotus corniculatus. Crobh Éin (Sicíní, Pabhsaer na Cuaiche)* 3.51

Bird's-foot Trefoil is particularly abundant in Aran and is one of the nine 'core species' of machairs. It can be seen carpeting the ground with its bright yellow flowers in spring and early summer. As a legume, it can fix atmospheric nitrogen and thus improve soil fertility.

The name Bird's-foot Trefoil derives from the distinctive 'bird's-foot' appearance of the mature seed pods (25–30 mm long) and its mainly trifoliate leaves. However, it has at least 70 other local names in English. The flowers are pea-like, bright yellow, 10–15 mm long, in clusters of 3–6.

Thrift (Sea Pink, Lady's Cushion). *Armeria maritima. Rabhán (Nóinín an Chladaigh, Pabhsaer Barr Aille)* 3.52

The familiar and distinctive Thrift is a Western-Atlantic species, abundant on rocky foreshores and cliff tops throughout Ireland. Pollen records show that this species has been established in Ireland since late-glacial times (12,000 years ago).

3.51 Bird's-foot Trefoil; 3.52 Thrift

Clockwise from top: **3.53** Sea Campion; **3.54** Rock Samphire; **3.55** Biting Stonecrop

The leaves are dark green, linear (grass-like), about 20 mm long, forming dense hummocks or cushions. The flowers are bright pink, 5-petalled, in round papery heads on stems up to 20 cm tall.

Sea Campion (Bladder Campion). *Silene vulgaris* subsp. *maritima*. *Coireán Mara*[3.53]

Sea Campion is a perennial herb, abundant in all the coastal habitats of Ireland. It can be recognized by its striped swollen calyx below the open flowers.

The leaves are opposite, grey-green, fleshy, elliptical, up to 20 mm long. The flowers appear from June to August and are 18–30 mm across, pure white, with 5 petals, each 2-lobed.

Rock Samphire. *Crithmum maritimum*. *Craobhraic*[3.54]

Rock Samphire is a perennial herb, occasional to frequent in Aran on shingle and rocks within reach of sea spray. Although it grows up to 30 cm on mainland coasts, in Aran the winds usually limit its height to below 10 cm (Wright 1866). This aromatic plant was recorded by O'Flaherty 'in plenty' in 1684, particularly on Oileán Dá Bhranóg. It was exported regularly to Dublin in the nineteenth century for use in pickles and preserves (O'Donovan 1839).

The leaves are antler-like, succulent and fleshy, greyish-green, with almost cylindrical segments 10–40 mm long. The flowers are small, greenish-yellow, in flat-topped clusters (umbels) about 60 mm across.

Biting Stonecrop. *Sedum acre*. *Grafán Buí na gCloch (Púirín Seangán)*[3.55]

Biting Stonecrop is very common in sandy areas in Aran. Ant colonies frequently occur under this plant, hence one of its Irish synonyms, *Púirín Seangán* (*púirín* means a small shelter or hutch and *seangán* is an ant). In folk medicine it is used to treat warts.

Its stems are prostrate, bearing leaves 5 mm long, ovoid, bluntly pointed, with a peppery taste. The flowers are bright yellow, 5-petalled, 15 mm across.

Sea Bindweed. *Calystegia soldanella*. *Plúr an Phrionsa*[3.56]

Sea Bindweed is found occasionally around the Irish coastline and is locally abundant in the Aran sand dunes.

3.56 Sea Bindweed

This plant figures prominently in the Jacobite folklore of Ireland and Scotland. The name in Irish derives from the Scots Gaelic *Flùr a' Phrionnsa* (The Flower of the Prince). It grows on the beach at Coilleag a' Phrionnsa, Eriskay, Western Isles of Scotland (Hebrides),[3.57] the spot where Bonnie Prince Charlie landed from France to start the 1745 rebellion. There are many versions in Scottish folklore as to how he may have planted or dropped seeds of the plant there. It is a common belief in the Western Isles that *Flùr a' Phrionnsa* grows nowhere else but on Eriskay (Cooper 1977).

Sea Bindweed is a low-growing perennial with underground creeping stems. The leaves are on long stalks, kidney-shaped, up to 40 mm across, bright green and succulent. The solitary flowers are prominent, trumpet-shaped, pale pink with white stripes, about 40 mm across.

Sea-kale (Sea Cabbage). *Crambe maritima. Praiseach Thrá*[3.58]
Sea-kale has been recorded in Aran from as far back as the late seventeenth century (O'Flaherty 1684). It was found there intermittently in the nineteenth century (O'Flaherty 1824; Wright 1866) and was rediscovered in 1972. It was formerly a Protected Species in the Irish Republic, at a time

when it was more widely collected as a vegetable. Nowadays its main threat is from recreational activities.

Sea-kale is most often found on rocky foreshores (such as near the Inis Meáin slip and at Loch Dearg, Inis Mór). The leaves are large and fleshy, somewhat waxy, pale bluish-green (cabbage-like). The flowers are white, 10–15 mm across in large panicles. The fruits are round and 1-seeded. As a brassica it has many culinary uses, particularly in salads.

Sea-holly. *Eryngium maritimum. Cuileann Trá*[3.59]
Sea-holly is a distinctive bushy perennial, 30–50 cm high, locally frequent on the dunes in Aran. It was recorded in Aran as far back as 1684 by

Clockwise from top: **3.57** Sea Bindweed at Coilleag a' Phrionnsa, Eriskay, Scotland; **3.58** Sea-kale; **3.59** Sea-holly

3.60 Kidney Vetch; 3.61 Sea Beet; 3.62 Dune stabilized with Marram, Inis Oírr

Roderic O'Flaherty and was used in folk medicine, particularly for treating worms in children (Ó Síocháin 1962).

The leaves are bluish-green, broad and very prickly. The flowers are pale blue, in dense globular heads.

Kidney Vetch. *Anthyllis vulneraria. Méara Muire*[3.60]

Kidney Vetch is a prostrate leguminous herb, common around the Irish coast and abundant in Aran. It is well known in folk medicine for healing wounds and for treating kidney disorders.

The leaves bear 7–15 narrow elliptical leaflets and are covered with silky hairs. The individual flowers are yellow, 12–15 mm long, borne in clover-like heads up to 40 mm across, on long stems.

Sea Beet. *Beta vulgaris* subsp. *maritima. Laíon na Trá*[3.61]

Sea Beet is an Atlantic species, common on rocky coastlines in Ireland and frequent in Aran. It is an ancestor of the cultivated sugar beet and its thick juicy leaves can be used in salads.

Sea Beet is a large perennial plant with sprawling stems up to 100 cm long. The leaves are stalked, shiny dark-green, oval to triangular and fleshy. The flowers are green at first, in terminal spikes, turning brown with seed set.

Marram. *Ammophila arenaria. Muiríneach*[3.62]

Marram is a salt-tolerant grass, abundant in the Cill Éinne dunes on Inis Mór and local elsewhere. It was once used for thatching. It has been planted in Inis Meáin and Inis Oírr to stabilize dunes. It is a 'pioneer plant' since it is often the first to colonize bare sand. Its upwardly growing rhizomes allow it to adapt to continuously rising sand levels.

Lichens

Lichens thrive on the Aran rocks, whether on the limestone clints, the stone walls or the glacial erratics. They also colonize the twigs of bushes such as Hawthorn. Their prevalence is due to the moist atmosphere and the exceptionally clean air that has been 'scrubbed' of contaminants by rainfall over thousands of kilometres of the Atlantic. The Aran Islands are unlikely to experience a level of human activity that would seriously affect the lichen flora (McCarthy & Mitchell 1988). This contrasts with the Burren

3.63 Profuse lichen growth, Dún Chonchúir, Inis Meáin; 3.64 Sparse lichen growth, Dublin city centre

mainland where acidic precipitation from industrialization of the Shannon estuary can limit lichen growth.

Lichens and mosses are very sensitive to air pollution and are good bio-indicators of sulphur dioxide (SO_2). White and orange lichens (*Aspicula* and *Caloplaca* spp.) are particularly profuse in Aran and add colour to the stone walls and ancient ruins.[3.63] In contrast, air pollution combined with a drier climate limits lichen growth in eastern urban areas of Ireland.[3.64]

Lichens comprise a unique algal/fungal combination, rather like a sandwich with the alga as the filling. Hundreds of species have been identified in Ireland, up to twenty of which are unique to The Burren and Aran (McCarthy & Mitchell 1988). In appearance, they are of three main types: 1) Crustose – flat, like stains on the limestone clints; 2) Foliose – leafy-edged; and 3) Fruticose – in ragged tufts, as found on twigs. Although common in Aran, their growth rates are fairly slow, with the crustose colonies on the clints only expanding by up to 2 mm per annum. These crustose species cause pitting of the clint surfaces, which eventually leads to the formation of solution hollows where higher plants may establish.

In Aran, lichens colonize the glacial erratics extensively, particularly those composed of granite. Granite consists of three minerals (quartz, mica and feldspar), compared with only one in limestone (calcium carbonate), and is thus a richer source of nutrients. Lichens (and mosses) also grow more profusely on the north-easterly sides of erratics, where they have more protection from the drying effects of the sun and the prevailing south-westerly winds.[1.13]

Lichens (*crotal* in Irish) were used in Aran to dye wool up to the early twentieth century. Three main types were used – *crotal buí* (yellow), *crotal dubh* (black) and *crotal geal* (white). The colours required were determined by the acidy of the mix in the dyepot and various ingredients were added to achieve the desired hues.

Algae and Cyanobacteria

Marine algae (seaweeds) are described in Chapter 5.

Algal paper. *Oedogonium* spp.[3.65]

At the edges of shallow turloughs in Aran and The Burren an extensive off-white slimy mass may be seen covering the vegetation, particularly after periods of warm dry weather. This is the dried and filamentous remains of algae, known as 'algal paper' and consisting of various species of the genus *Oedogonium* (Chlorophyceae) (Scannell 1972; Reynolds 1983). In Aran, it has been noted on Inis Mór and Inis Meáin (at Loch Mhuirbhigh, a placename common to both islands).

Algal paper appears in other similar limestone areas of Europe. In Germany it is known as 'meteorpapier': it may seem to have appeared overnight because of its rapid growth.

Nostoc spp.[3.66]

The solution hollows in the limestone pavements of Aran often contain dark jelly-like masses of a cyanobacterium (*Nostoc* spp., also classified as Blue-green Algae). This genus secretes a weak acid, which dissolves out depressions in the limestone clints ('giant's footprints'). In droughty periods it dries out into black powdery granules.

In the deeper solution hollows, residues of *Nostoc* can initiate the process of soil formation, with later colonization by mosses and higher plants. In some conditions, this new 'soil' can be acidic rather than alkaline and supports calcifuge (lime-hating) plants such as heathers.[3.23]

In folk medicine, *Nostoc* has been used for treating burns.

 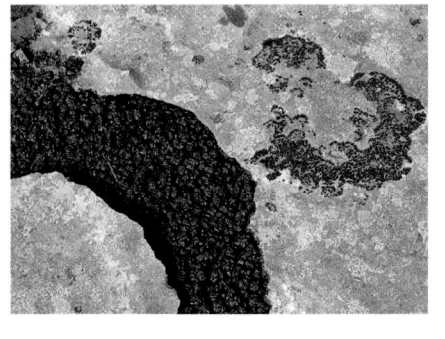

3.65 Algal paper; 3.66 *Nostoc*

Fauna

4

As I lie here hour after hour, I seem to enter into the wild pastime of the cliff, and to become a companion of the cormorants and crows.

J.M. Synge, The Aran Islands

The Aran Islands have an interesting range of birds, mammals and insects, most of which are also common throughout the Irish mainland. However, due to their relative isolation and island status some species of the mainland fauna (such as foxes, hares and frogs) are absent. As it would be impracticable to include in this *Nature Guide* the thousands of species comprising the entire Aran fauna, only those that are common and likely to be seen by visitors are described.

Birdlife

The Aran Islands support a large and varied population of sea and coastal birds but comparatively few passerines (perching songbirds). Many of the species are listed under Annex I of the European Birds Directive. Species common along the west coast are also prevalent in Aran, but the number and diversity of birds are lower than in other Galway islands (Hutchinson 1986). The Aran cliffs are generally too sheer to provide good nesting sites. In the past, sea birds were a resource to be exploited by the islanders as food, oil for lamps and feathers for pillows and mattresses (O'Flaherty 1684; O'Flaherty 1991).

The birds described below are limited to the nineteen species that are particularly associated with Aran, most of which breed there, and are likely to be noticed by visitors (List 1, Notable land birds, and List 3, Notable sea and shore birds). The forty-two other breeding land and sea birds recorded for Aran, most of which are common and well-known throughout Ireland, are also noted but are not described (Lists 2 and 4). In all, these Aran birds comprise about a third of all breeding Irish species.

The descriptions given here of the more notable Aran birds are largely derived from the *The Guide to the Birds of Ireland* (D'Arcy 1981), *The Complete Guide to Irish Birds* (Dempsey & O'Clery 1993) and *Ireland's Bird Life* (Lansdown 1994). The overall list of breeding birds is derived from *An Atlas of Breeding Birds of The Burren and the Aran Islands* (Lysaght 2002) and *The Atlas of Breeding Birds in Britain and Ireland* (Sharrock 1976).

The number of breeding birds recorded for Aran has grown gradually over the centuries. Patrick Pearse compiled more than twenty names in Irish of birds on Inis Meáin in the 1890s. *The Atlas of Breeding Birds in Britain and Ireland* (Sharrock 1976) suggested more than fifty breeding species. A survey in winter 1957 listed fifty-two species on Inis Mór. The latest estimate (Lysaght 2002) is for sixty breeding species on the islands.

A number of species no longer breed in Aran, although they may occasionally stray in from the mainland. These include the Corncrake, Corn Bunting, Dunlin, Puffin and Peregrine Falcon.

LAND BIRDS
1. Notable land birds

Cuckoo. *Cuculus canorus. Cuach* [4.1]

The Cuckoo is a summer migrant to Ireland from southern and eastern Africa. It is a long-tailed species with bluish-grey upperparts, dark-barred white underparts and pointed (hawk-like) wingtips. The distinctive call of the male bird can be heard throughout Aran in the summer. The females, though rarely heard, give a longer, bubbling call. They lay their eggs in the nests of host species such as Meadow Pipit and Dunnock, and often eat or throw out any existing eggs.

The young Cuckoos born in Aran, who have never made the journey south, nevertheless migrate successfully to Africa in autumn a few weeks ahead of their parents.

4.1 Cuckoo

4.2 Meadow Pipit

Meadow Pipit. *Anthus pratensis. Riabhóg Mhóna* [4.2]

The Meadow Pipit is widespread in Aran and throughout Ireland. It is a small streaked brownish bird (somewhat like a miniature thrush) with pale orange legs and a distinctive thin *tseep-tseep-tseep* call.

This bird is also called *Giolla na Cuaiche* (Cuckoo's Gillie) in Irish, since the Cuckoo frequently lays its eggs in the Meadow Pipit's nest. Flocks of Meadow Pipits may occasionally be seen mobbing a Cuckoo to drive it away from their nests.

Chough. *Pyrrhocorax pyrrhocorax. Cág Cosdearg* [4.3]

The Chough is a jackdaw-sized glossy black bird. It was first noted in Aran (as the 'Cornish Crow') by Roderic O'Flaherty in 1684. Although it is the rarest member of the crow family in Ireland, it nevertheless comprises 70 per cent of the entire north-west European population (Gray *et al.* 2003). It is at the northerly and westerly limit of its global range, has Protected status throughout Ireland and is listed in *The Irish Red Data Book* (Whilde 1993).

The Chough has a distinctive long, curved, red bill and red legs and is noted for its acrobatic flight. It has a loud, high-pitched *chauuh* or *kee-ow* call. It is a 'maritime' crow, found nesting almost exclusively in rocky

Clockwise from top left: **4.3** Chough; **4.4** Skylark; **4.5** Wheatear

crevices or cliffs around the south, west and north coasts of Ireland (Bullock *et al.* 1983).

Choughs can be seen feeding on insects in the machairs and close-grazed fields of Aran. A fall in the chough population on Inis Mór over the past decade may be linked to reduced grazing intensity in the pastures (Gray *et al.* 2003).

Skylark. *Alauda arvensis. Fuiseog*[4.4]

The Skylark has mottled brownish upper parts, creamy underparts and a distinctive crest on the head, which can be flattened or raised. The male is a tireless singer, delivering its loud chirrup for hours while fluttering high over its territory.

The Skylark is more often heard than seen, but with careful stalking can be observed ground-feeding on grasslands. It is one of the first birds the visitor to Aran may hear in summer. However, the newly arrived visitor will only hear it after the noisy planes or boats have departed and the customary stillness of the islands has resumed.

Wheatear. *Oenanthe oenanthe. Clochrán*[4.5]

The Wheatear is a summer visitor to Aran from equatorial Africa, traditionally arriving around St Patrick's Day. It has a white rump (obvious when flying away) and a black inverted T on a short white tail. Its call is a short harsh *chack* or *wee-chack*.

The name 'Wheatear' refers neither to wheat nor to ears but is derived from Old English 'hwit' (white) and 'aers' (arse).

Lapwing (Green Plover). *Vanellus vanellus. Pilibín*[4.6]

The Lapwing is a distinctive black-and-white plover, common in Aran and throughout Ireland on grasslands and wetlands. In summer the males bear a long crest on the head. Its distinctive call is a loud excited *pee-weet*.

Ringed Plover. *Charadrius hiaticula. Feadóg Chladaigh*[4.7]

The ringed plover is common on the machairs on Inis Mór and Inis Meáin.

4.6 Lapwing; 4.7 Ringed Plover

4.8 Corncrake

It is a small, lively, plump, brown-and-white wader, with a distinctive black 'ringed' breastband, a striking face pattern and bright orange legs. Its call is a distinctive fluty *too-ip*. Its nest is a mere shallow depression in the ground and is thus very vulnerable to human interference.

Corncrake. *Crex crex. Traonach*[4.8]

Although currently absent from Aran, the Corncrake was a common summer visitor there from central Africa up to the late 1980s. Its distribution is now mainly confined to the Shannon callows, north Donegal, west Mayo and Connemara. It is threatened with global extinction and is listed in *The Irish Red Data Book* (Whilde 1993). The more than 80 per cent decline in Corncrake numbers between 1988 and 1993 is usually blamed on modern farming methods, particularly silage-making. However, this does not explain its disappearance from areas such as Aran where only traditional farming is practiced.

The last calling male was recorded on Inis Meáin during the National Corncrake Survey in 1993. However, various conservation measures by the

Department of the Environment, BirdWatch Ireland and the EU REPS scheme have resulted in a small but encouraging increase in Corncrake numbers in Donegal, Mayo and some islands off the west coast in 2003–5. If such progress is maintained, this shy and elusive bird may yet return to Aran.

The Corncrake is a dumpy brownish bird, about 27 cm long, more often heard than seen. It has streaked and barred upperparts, chestnut-coloured wings and light underparts. The male call is unmistakable – striking at first but irritating when repeated all night. It is a very distinctive loud, harsh *kerrx-kerrx* sound (from which *Crex* is derived).

2. Other land birds recorded in Aran

Robin. *Erithacus rubecula. Spideog*

Wren. *Troglodytes troglodytes. Dreoilín*

Blackbird. *Turdus merula. Lon Dubh*

Song Thrush. *Turdus philomelos. Smólach*

Mistle Thrush. *Turdus viscivorus. Liatráisc (Smólach Mór)*

Goldfinch. *Carduelis carduelis. Lasair Choille*

Pied Wagtail. *Motacilla alba. Glasóg Shráide*

Swift. *Apus apus. Gabhlán Gaoithe*
On Inis Mór only.

Swallow. *Hirunda rustica. Fáinleog*

House Martin. *Delichon urbica. Gabhlán Binne*
On Inis Oírr only.

Starling. *Sturnus vulgaris. Druid*

House Sparrow. *Passer domesticus. Gealbhan Binne*

Dunnock. *Prunella modularis. Bráthair an Dreoilín (Donnóg)*

Linnet. *Carduelis cannabina. Gleoiseach*

Rock Pipit. *Anthus petrosus. Riabhóg Chladaigh*

Stonechat. *Saxicola torquata. Caislín (Cloch) Aitinn*

Whitethroat. *Sylvia communis. Gilphíb Phíoba*
On Inis Mór only.

Chiffchaff. *Phylloscopus collybita. Tiuf-teaf*

Sedge Warbler. *Acrocephalus schoenobaenus. Ceolaire Cíbe*
On Inis Meáin only.

Collared Dove. *Streptopelia decaocto. Fearán Baicdhubh*
Nesting in Ireland since 1959. In Cill Rónáin (Inis Mór) from about 1973.

Rock Dove. *Columba livia. Colm Aille*

Woodpigeon. *Columba palumbus. Colm Coille*

Redshank. *Tringa totanus. Cosdeargán*

Magpie. *Pica pica. Snag Breac*
On Inis Mór only.

Jackdaw. *Corvus monedula. Cág*

Hooded Crow. *Corvus corone cornix. Feannóg (Caróg Liath)*

Raven. *Corvus corax. Fiach Dubh*
On Inis Mór only.

Kestrel. *Falco tinnunculus. Pocaire Gaoithe*

Pheasant. *Phasianus colchicus. Piasún*
On Inis Mór only.

Curlew. *Numenius arquata. Crotach*
Winter visitor.

Grey Heron. *Ardea cinerea. Corr Réisc*

Moorhen. *Gallinula chloropus. Cearc Uisce*

Mute Swan. *Cygnus olor. Eala Bhalbh*

Shelduck. *Tadorna tadorna. Seil-lacha*

Mallard. *Anas platyrhynchos. Mallard*

Red-breasted Merganser. *Mergus serrator. Síolta Rua*

SEA AND SHORE BIRDS
3. Notable sea and shore birds

Cormorant. *Phalacrocorax carbo. Broigheall*[4.9]
The Cormorant is a very distinctive and conspicuous species, common around the Irish coast and on large inland lakes. It is a large, heavily built bird, dark-coloured, with yellow around the eyes. The adults have white facial and thigh patches in the breeding season. In Aran they are found around Inis Mór and Inis Meáin but do not breed there.

Cormorants fly low over the water with quick wing beats. They are often seen standing with wings outstretched on rocky promontories. This stance was long assumed to aid drying of the wings after diving, but is now thought to have a digestive function.

Shag. *Phalacrocorax aristotelis. Seaga (Cailleach Dhubh)*
The Shag is a smaller version of the Cormorant, and breeds on all three of the Aran Islands. In summer it bears a distinctive crest on the head. It has a more greenish-black colour and is darker around the eyes than the Cormorant.

The local Aran name for the Shag is *Cailleach Dhubh*, a term rare in

4.9 Cormorant; **4.10** Gannets

Irish/English dictionaries and usually translated as 'Cormorant'. In J.M. Synge's play *Riders to the Sea* about an Aran boating tragedy, *Cailleach Dhubh* is translated literally as 'black hag', as in 'isn't it a bitter thing to think of him floating that way to the far north, and no one to keen him but the black hags that do be flying on the sea'.

Gannet. *Sula bassana (Morus bassanus). Gainéad* [4.10]

The Gannet is Ireland's largest breeding seabird, with a wingspan of up to 2 m. It is a common bird of the open sea. It does not breed on Aran but only on a few isolated islands such as the Skelligs, the Saltees, Bull Rock and Clare Island. The Skelligs have almost 30,000 apparently occupied sites (AOS), reputedly the second-largest colony in the world after St Kilda in Scotland (182,000 AOS).

The adult birds can be readily distinguished by their long, brilliant white, black-tipped wings, cigar-shaped body, creamy-yellow head and spear-like bill. They catch fish by making spectacular dives into the sea from heights of up to 40 m.

Guillemot. *Uria aalge. Foracha (An tÉan Aille)* [4.11]

The Guillemot spends its life at sea, only coming ashore to breed. It is a slim auk with a dark, dagger-like bill and dark legs. Its head and upperparts are dark chocolate-brown in summer, with white underparts (somewhat like a small penguin).

Guillemots form extremely noisy and crowded colonies on open rocky ledges, emitting harsh, rolling *oarr* calls. They appear to have increased recently in Aran, with more than 3000 individuals recorded in 1999.

4.11 Guillemots

Guillemots were once much sought after by the islanders for their flesh and feathers (O'Flaherty 1991). They were netted on the ledges of high cliffs, plucked, salted and packed in barrels.

Razorbill. *Alca torda. Crosán*[4.12]

The Razorbill is an auk, somewhat similar in appearance to the Guillemot. However, its upperparts are black and, in contrast to the Guillemot's pointed dagger-like bill, its bill is more massive and blunt, with a distinctive white stripe towards the tip.

Razorbills are much less common in Aran than Guillemots (about 300, compared to more than 3000 of the latter). They breed only on Inis Mór, on the cliffs at Dún Dúchathair and west of Dún Aonghasa at the eponymous Ulán na gCrosán (Boulder of the Razorbills).

Kittiwake. *Rissa tridactyla. Saidhbhéar*[4.13]

The Kittiwake is a familiar gull, breeding around the cliffs and caves of the Irish coast, and common in Aran. In appearance it is rather like the common gull, but smaller. It is the most truly oceanic of Irish breeding gulls, spending the winter months as far out as Greenland and Newfoundland. On Inis Mór, 820 breeding pairs were recorded in a 1970 survey.

The Kittiwake is a slender bird showing long, pointed, distinctly black-tipped wings in flight. The upperparts of summer adults are dark grey and the underparts and head are white. The call is a loud, repeated *kitti-waak*, usually only heard on the breeding cliffs.

Fulmar. *Fulmarus glacialis. Fulmaire*[4.14]

The Fulmar spends its first 3–4 years wandering throughout the North Atlantic, after which it only comes ashore to breed. It was first recorded in Ireland in the early twentieth century, and has been recorded nesting since 1911. Since then, numbers have grown spectacularly to about 20,000 pairs. In Aran it breeds on Inis Mór and Inis Meáin.

The name 'Fulmar' originated in the Western Isles of Scotland. Since it did not reach our shores until the early twentieth century and therefore had no traditional name in Irish, 'Fulmar' was simply translated to *Fulmaire*.

Though members of the petrel family, Fulmars are quite gull-like in appearance and colour (grey and white), with thickset necks and long, narrow, stiff wings. They have thick, tube-nosed, yellowish bills. The legs are set

4.12 Razorbills; **4.13** Kittiwakes

4.14 Fulmar; **4.15** Common Sandpiper

well back and are incapable of supporting the bird in a standing position. They can be seen riding the updrafts on cliff faces, cruising apparently effortlessly with only occasional wing-beats.

Common Sandpiper. *Actitis hypoleuca. Gobadán* [4.15]
The Common Sandpiper is a small, brown-backed, white-bellied shore
wader with a constantly bobbing head and long tail. It is a summer visitor
to Aran from Africa, with a distinctive *swee-wee-wee* call.

The Common Sandpiper can be seen busily foraging near the water's
edge. Its feeding habit gave rise to the well-known Irish proverb *Ní féidir
leis an ngobadán an dá thrá a fhreastal*, meaning 'the sandpiper can't work
two strands at the same time', i.e. you can only do one thing at a time.

TERNS

Terns are small graceful seabirds, often described as 'sea swallows'. They are
distributed around the Irish coast (mostly on offshore islands) and on large
inland lakes (Hannon *et al.* 1998). They dive into the surf to feed on small
fish such as sand-eels. They have harsh strident calls and may attack animals
and people coming too close to their nests. The nests are mere depressions
scraped out of the sand and are very vulnerable to disturbance by vehicles,
livestock and human activities such as walking, shore angling and swimming.
There are five tern species in Ireland, three of which breed in Aran and are
described below.

Arctic Tern. *Sterna paradisaea. Geabhróg Artach* [4.16]
The Arctic Tern is one of the world's great travellers, clocking up to 40,000
km each year. Its breeding range extends north above the Arctic Circle and
it can travel as far south as the Antarctic. Their seasonal migrations follow
the sun to high latitudes and consequently they live in almost continuous
daylight.

The Arctic Tern has a blood-red bill (with no black tip). About 3000
pairs breed on undisturbed islands off Ireland's west coast. They arrive in
Aran from late April to early May and breed on all three islands, with their
largest colony (more than 300 pairs) on An tOileán Iatharach off Inis Mór.

Little Tern. *Sterna albifrons. Geabhróg Bheag*
Little Terns are not only the smallest of the Irish terns but also comprise
the smallest population of any of our breeding seabirds. Numbers have
declined by one-third in recent years (Hannon *et al.* 1998). They are a
Protected Species throughout Ireland (Whilde 1993) and are included in
the Irish Amber List of threatened species.

4.16 Arctic Tern

Little Terns have yellow legs and (in the breeding season) black-tipped yellow bills and white foreheads. They arrive in late April to early May from West Africa and breed on all three of the islands.

The small colony on Inis Meáin (about fifteen pairs) is a very important habitat for this threatened species, as it comprises 5–10 per cent of the entire national population. The islanders on Inis Meáin and Inis Mór have implemented conservation schemes to protect the nesting sites against human disturbance.

Sandwich Tern. *Sterna sandvicensis. Geabhróg Scothdhubh*
The Sandwich Tern is the largest and most gull-like of the Aran terns. It has a black bill with a yellow tip, black legs and a shaggy crest. Small numbers breed on Inis Mór and Inis Oírr.

4. Other sea and shore birds recorded in Aran

Common Gull. *Larus canus. Faoileán Bán*

Black-headed Gull. *Larus ridibundus. Faoileán Ceanndubh (Sléibhín)*

Herring Gull. *Larus argentatus. Faoileán Scadán*

Great Black-backed Gull. *Larus marinus. Cóbach (Droimneach Mór)*
On Inis Mór only.

Black Guillemot. *Cepphus grylle. Foracha Dhubh*

Oystercatcher. *Haematopus ostralegus. Roilleach*

Mammals

Pygmy Shrew. *Sorex minutus. Dallóg Fhraoigh*
The Pygmy Shrew is the only shrew in Ireland and is the country's smallest mammal. It is an unexpected survivor from before the last Ice Age. Weighing only about 5 grams, and 50–65 mm in length, it is much smaller than the House Mouse. It is smoky-brown in colour and has a pointed, typically twitching nose. Due to its small size and furtive nature it is not noticed very often, but may occasionally be seen as 'road-kill'.

Otter. *Lutra lutra. Madra Uisce*
Otters had been occasionally noted swimming ashore in Aran but were not regarded as established inhabitants until recently. One was recovered from a lobster pot off Inis Mór in 1970 (Fairley 1975). In the 1970s Otter footprints were seen on Oileán na Tuí, Inis Mór (Robinson 1986) and on Ceann Gainimh, Inis Meáin. A survey in 1996–7, however, showed that they were well established along the north-east shore of Inis Mór (Kingston *et al.* 1999).

OTHER MAMMALS RECORDED IN ARAN
House Mouse. *Mus musculus. Luch*

Field Mouse. *Apodemus sylvaticus. Luch Fhéir*

Brown Rat. *Rattus norvegicus. Francach*

Bat. *Chiroptera. Sciathán Leathair*

Stoat. *Mustela erminea. Easóg*
On Inis Mór only.

Rabbit. *Oryctolagus cuniculus. Coinín*

EXTINCT MAMMALS
Hares
Previously noted as 'abundant' by O'Flaherty (1824) and by Lewis (1837).

Foxes

Reptiles

Viviparous Lizard (Common Lizard). *Lacerta vivipara. Earc Luachra*
The Viviparous Lizard is Ireland's only native lizard. Its species name *vivipara* means that the female retains the eggs inside her body until they hatch. It varies in length from 10 to 20 cm and is usually well camouflaged against its surroundings, having a yellowish-brown or greyish colour with irregular dark markings. It hibernates from October to March.

The Viviparous Lizard is very elusive and can only be observed if approached quietly and unobtrusively. It is most likely to be seen in Aran during sunny periods, basking on the rocks in sheltered spots. Like all reptiles, it is cold-blooded but can move quickly when sufficiently warmed up.

Amphibians

In common with many of Ireland's offshore islands, no frogs have been recorded in Aran to date. Newts are also absent.

Insects

Although the number of insect species in Aran is less than on the mainland, the more colourful types are, like the wild flowers, particularly striking against the grey limestone backdrop.

BUMBLE BEES. *BOMBUS* SPP. *BUMBÓG*
About twenty species of bumble bees have been recorded to date in Ireland.

Aran, however, has its own distinctive subspecies, *Bombus muscorum smithianus* (Stelfox 1933). This was first discovered in Aran in 1931 and was also recorded from the Scilly Isles, the Shetlands, the Western Isles (Hebrides) and northern Norway. As its name suggests, it is closely related to the common Bumble Bee (or Moss Carder, *Bombus muscorum*), which occurs on the Irish mainland and occasionally in Aran.

In contrast to the mainland Bumble Bee, which has an all-over rusty-blonde colour, the Aran subspecies has predominantly dark hairs on the underside. It lives in sandy soil, forms nests in meadows and is commonly seen on brambles, Knapweed and Fuchsia in mid- to late summer (Breen 2004).

BUTTERFLIES

The low-intensity farming system in Aran, together with the limited herbicide and pesticide use, results in a diverse flora, favouring butterflies and day-flying moths. Their caterpillars, in particular, are often associated with specific host plants and this can help in species identification. Nineteen resident butterflies have been recorded in Aran to date, together with two summer migrants to Ireland. The range of species is similar, though somewhat fewer in number, to that found in limestone areas of the mainland such as The Burren.

The descriptions below are based largely on those in *Complete Irish Wildlife* (Sterry 2004) and *Butterflies* (Chinery 2004). Sizes are given as the average length in mm of a single forewing measured from the shoulder to the wingtip, and occurrence as: A = recorded on Inis Mór; M = Inis Meáin; and O = Inis Oírr.

FAMILY PIERIDAE

Brimstone. *Gonepteryx rhamni. Buíóg Ruibheach. 30 mm. AMO* [4.17]
Emerge from February onwards on sunny days. Have uniquely shaped wings and the males are a distinctive brimstone-yellow or sulphur colour. Caterpillars feed on Buckthorn (*Rhamnus cathartica*).

Small White. *Pieris rapae. Bánóg Bheag. 25 mm. AO*
A common species in gardens. Their caterpillars are a troublesome pest of brassicas. Females have two black spots on uppersides of creamy-white forewings, while males have only one. Underwings yellowish.

4.17 Brimstone

Large White. *Pieris brassicae. Bánóg Mhór. 32 mm. AO*[4.18]
Well-known as the 'Cabbage White'. Its yellow and black caterpillars feed on brassicas. Females have black spots on the creamy-white uppersides of the wings, absent in males. Underwings yellowish.

Green-veined White. *Pieris napi. Bánóg Uaine. 25 mm. AO*[4.19]
Similar to Small White but veins are dark on upperwings and greyish-green on underwings. Females have two black spots on the forewing uppersides, while males have only one.

Orange-tip. *Anthocharis cardamines. Barr Buí. 23 mm. AO*[4.20]
The orange tips of the male wings are unmistakable. In contrast, females lack orange tips and have a solid black patch on the wing upperside. Hind underwings of both sexes marbled green and white. Caterpillars feed on Cuckoo-flower (*Cardamine pratensis*).

FAMILY LYCANIDAE
Small Blue. *Cupido minimus. Gormán Beag. 12 mm. AMO*[4.21]
Small and highly active, particularly in June–July. Caterpillars feed on Kidney Vetch. Male wings show purplish iridescence, with grey underwings.

Clockwise from top left: **4.18** Large White; **4.19** Green-veined White; **4.20** Orange-tip; **4.21** Small Blue

4.22 Common Blue

Common Blue. *Polyommatus icarus. Gormán Coiteann. 17 mm.* AMO^{4.22}

Male upperwings blue, females generally brown. Underwings grey-brown with dark spots. Caterpillars feed on Bird's-foot Trefoil (*Lotus corniculatus*).

Small Copper. *Lycaena phlaeas. Copróg Bheag. 14 mm. AO*
Showing bright coppery forewings when basking. Broad dark border and irregular black spots on outer forewings.

FAMILY NYMPHALIDAE
Small Tortoiseshell. *Aglais (Nymphalis) urticae. Ruán Beag. 25 mm.* AMO^{4.23}

Common sun-loving garden species, March–October. Upperwings marbled orange, yellow and black; underparts smoky-brown. Caterpillars feed on Common Nettle (*Urtica dioica*).

Peacock. *Inachis io. Péacóg. 30 mm. AO*
Maroon upperwings have bold and colourful eye markings to deter predators. Caterpillars feed on Common Nettle (*Urtica dioica*).

Dark Green Fritillary. *Argynnis (Mesoacidalia) aglaia. Fritileán Dúghlas. 30 mm. AMO*[4.24]
Orange-brown uppersides with variable pattern of black spots. Greenish on undersides, with silver spots. Caterpillars feed on violets (*Viola* spp.).

Marsh Fritillary. *Euphydryas aurinia. Fritileán Réisc. 40–50 mm. A*[4.25]
Wings marked with orange and yellow bands. Distinct row of black spots on both sides of hindwing. Caterpillars feed on Devil's-bit Scabious (*Succisa pratensis*). Protected under Annex II of the EU Habitats Directive.

Migrants
Red Admiral. *Vanessa atalanta. Aimiréal Dearg. 30 mm. AO*
Mainly a summer migrant to Ireland. Distinct velvety black uppersides, with red and white markings. Underwings marbled smoky-grey. Caterpillars feed on Common Nettle (*Urtica dioica*).

Painted Lady. *Vanessa (Cynthia) cardui. Áilleán. 30 mm. AO*
A summer migrant to Ireland from North Africa. Seen basking with wings

4.23 Small Tortoiseshell; **4.24** Dark Green Fritillary

wide open. Upperwings marbled pinkish buff, white and black. Round black dots near edges of hindwings. Caterpillars feed on thistles.

FAMILY SATYRIDAE

Speckled Wood. *Pararge aegeria. Breachfhéileacán. 21 mm. AO*
Cream spots on brown upperwings. Often seen basking on sun-dappled leaves with wings open.

Wall Brown. *Lasiommata megera. Donnóg an Bhalla. 23 mm. AO*[4.26]
Found in grasslands and rough ground. Wing uppersides orange-brown with pale yellow patches and small eyespots.

4.25 Marsh Fritillary

4.26 Wall Brown; 4.27 Grayling

Grayling. *Hipparchia semele. Glasán. 20–30 mm. AO*[4.27]
Well-camouflaged when settled on ground with wings closed and oriented
to minimize shadow. Uppersides dull brown with paler bands at edges. Two
eyespots on forewings.

Meadow Brown. *Maniola jurtina. Donnóg Fhéir. 25 mm. AO*
Found in grasslands. Male uppersides are dark brown with faint orange
smudges and eyespot. Undersides of forewings largely orange in both sexes.

Ringlet. *Aphantopus hyperantus. Fáinneog. 19 mm. AO*[4.28]
Uppersides velvety smoky-brown, with small eyespots.

Small Heath. *Coenonympha pamphilus. Fraochán Beag.*
14–20 mm. AO[4.29]
Found in grasslands. Uppersides are orange-brown with grey margins and a
small eyespot at the tip. Undersides of forewing also largely orange, with a
prominent eyespot.

FAMILY HESPERIDAE

Dingy Skipper. *Erynnis tages. Donnán. 14 mm. A*[4.30]
Moth-like, with grey-brown upperwings and reddish-brown underwings.
In meadows and on rough ground. Caterpillars feed on Bird's-foot Trefoil
(*Lotus corniculatus*) and other legumes.

4.28 Ringlet; 4.29 Small Heath

MOTHS

Moths are generally slower-flying than butterflies and when at rest fold their wings in a tent-like manner. In the absence of detailed surveys, current information on the moths of the Aran Islands is fairly scant. A few day-flying moths (listed below) have been noted, mostly on Inis Meáin. Light-trapping would be required to collect and identify the night-flying species.

Magpie Moth. *Abraxas grossulariata. 22 mm*[4.31]
Distinctive black spots with wavy yellow stripe on white forewing. Black-spotted yellow abdomen.

In Aran, pupae form large colonies of spider-like webs on shrubs along walls.

Six-spot Burnet Moth. *Zygaena filipendulae. 11–18 mm*[4.32]
Slow, drifting flight. Dark forewings with usually six clear red spots. Hind-wings red with narrow black border. Pupates in papery cocoon attached to grass stems. Caterpillars feed on Bird's-foot Trefoil (*Lotus corniculatus*). The related species *Zygaena trifolii* has five spots.

Cinnabar Moth. *Tyria jacobaeae. 18 mm*[4.33]
Unmistakable with its charcoal-grey wings and red spots and red wing edges.

Single yellow cocoons found high up on grass stems. Caterpillars feed mainly on Ragwort (*Senecio jacobaea*).

Hummingbird Hawkmoth. *Macroglossum stellatarum. 23 mm*
Striking appearance and audible hum. Noticeable in hot dry weather, often as a migrant from continental Europe.

Clockwise from top left: **4.30** Dingy Skipper; **4.31** Magpie Moth; **4.32** Six-spot Burnet Moth

Forester Moth. *Adscita statices. 12 mm*

Forewing colours range from golden green to iridescent blue. Caterpillars feed mainly on Sorrel (*Rumex acetosa*).

Dew Moth. *Setina irrorella*

Rare. Recorded once on Inis Mór (Bond 2005).

4.33 Cinnabar Moth

Seashore

5

Did sea define the land or land the sea?
Each drew new meaning from the waves' collision.
Sea broke on land to full identity.

Seamus Heaney, 'Lovers on Aran'

The Aran Islands have much the same range of seashore animals and plants as are found along the rest of the west coast. However, the Purple Sea Urchin (*Paracentrotus lividus*), a sublittoral species common on the west coast from Kerry to Donegal, is particularly abundant on the exposed side of Inis Mór. Some rare species of soft corals, sea fans and anemones are also present in the reefs. The various forms of seashore life in Ireland have been well-documented in a range of publications (Challinor *et al.* 1999; McGrath 1984; Morrissey *et al.* 2001; Ní Nuadháin 1992).

Seaweeds

Seaweeds belong to the very diverse group of organisms collectively known as algae. Many algae contain chlorophyll, the pigment involved in photosynthesis, but its green colour is usually masked by other pigments. The three main seaweed types are the green algae (Chlorophyta), usually found in shallower waters, the brown algae (Phaeophyta, *feamainn dhubh/Feamainn Bhuí*) in the inter-tidal zone, and the red algae (Rhodophyta, *feamainn dhearg*) in deeper waters. In the clear waters of Aran, seaweeds are found as deep as 40 m.

Most Aran householders have land with access to the sea and still retain shore rights to gather seaweed. Its main uses were as fertilizer for crops and to 'make' land by mixing with sand,[6.4 6.7] and as the raw material for kelp manufacture. When seaweeds were more important in their economy, the islanders could identify and name in Irish some dozens of species. However, a combination of their lesser use and a possible decline in spoken Irish means that such local names may face extinction. This is well-expressed in Aidan Mathews' three-line poem, 'The Death of Irish' (1983):

> The tide gone out for good,
> Thirty-one words for seaweed
> Whiten on the foreshore.

As the traditional kelp industry declined in the mid-twentieth century, alternative uses for the abundant seaweeds around Galway Bay were investigated. The Industrial Research Council (later part of the Institute for Industrial Research & Standards, now Enterprise Ireland) sponsored commercial uses of seaweeds in cooperation with NUI Galway. The Galway researchers showed that seaweed derivatives had 'functional food'

5.1 Spiral Wrack

properties, for example as emulsifiers and thickening agents, and also had non-food applications in cosmetics and as gelling agents. One such derivative was alginic acid, a gel-forming polysaccharide first separated and identified from seaweed by Professor Tom Dillon in the 1940s. A group led by Professor Máirín de Valéra surveyed the seaweeds in the area, including the Aran Islands, in the 1950s (de Valéra 1958). They found that, compared to the mainland coastline, the Aran sites were not outstandingly rich in commercially important large seaweeds (kelps) or in edible species such as carrageen.

Arramara Teoranta was set up in Cill Chiaráin, Connemara, in 1947 to exploit seaweed products. It processes about 35,000 tonnes annually, mainly Knotted Wrack (*Ascophyllum nodosum, Feamainn Bhuí*) for animal feed supplements, soil conditioners and cosmetics, and alginates for the food industry. NUI Galway runs the Irish Seaweed Centre and AlgaeBase, a Global Species Database on algae. Enterprise Ireland (Biotechnology Directorate) supports research on potential therapeutic uses of seaweeds.

WRACKS (FUCOIDS)

These familiar seaweeds grow mostly on rocky shores, from the splash zone above high water down to low neap tide level. The different species (particularly in the genus *Fucus*) can be difficult to identify, since they frequently hybridize and their appearance also varies according to local conditions.

Spiral Wrack. *Fucus spiralis. Casfheamainn* [5.1]

Spiral Wrack is a brown alga with tough leathery fronds. It is somewhat like Bladderwrack (below) but without air bladders, and grows further up the shore in the upper zone. The fronds have a distinct midrib and tend to twist into a spiral shape, particularly when drying out. The fronds may bear swellings at their tips (not to be confused with the paired air bladders of Bladderwrack).

Knotted Wrack. *Ascophyllum nodosum. Feamainn Bhuí* [5.2]

Knotted Wrack (Egg Wrack) is a brown alga of the middle to upper zone, usually restricted to fairly sheltered sites. It is lighter in colour (olive-green to yellowy, hence *Feamainn Bhuí*) than most of the other 'brown' algae. The fronds are long (up to 2 m), somewhat flattened, leathery, bearing single egg-shaped air bladders at regular intervals. It is highly regarded ('*an sméar*

5.2 Knotted Wrack

5.3 Bladderwrack; 5.4 Serrated Wrack

mhullaigh', Mac an Iomaire 1985) as a fertilizer for the *garraithe* (potato 'gardens'). It contains high levels of nutrients, vitamins and trace elements and is the main species harvested commercially by Arramara Teoranta in the sheltered bays of Connemara.

Bladderwrack. *Fucus vesiculosus. Feamainn Bhoilgíneach* 5.3
Bladderwrack is a brown alga of the middle tidal zone, its colour varying from olive-brown to greenish-black to bright yellow. The numerous air

bladders found in pairs along the fronds give it its name. It is most common in the semi-sheltered conditions of inlets. It is used as a fertilizer, particularly for potatoes. In folk medicine it was used to treat rheumatism and, when well boiled and mashed to a jelly, was effective against some skin diseases.

Serrated Wrack. *Fucus serratus. Míoránach*[5.4]

Serrated Wrack is a common brown alga of the middle to lower shore. The fronds have characteristic saw-like (hence 'serrated') edges, are yellow-brown in colour and are irregularly branched. It is used in body-care products and thalassotherapy in Ireland, and in many other European countries.

KELP

Kelp is the calcined ashes of various large seaweeds, although the term is now more generally applied to the seaweeds themselves. The kelp industry started in Scotland about 1720 and flourished on-and-off in Aran into the twentieth century. It was particularly profitable in times of scarcity, such as the Napoleonic Wars and the World Wars. Kelp has a high content of sodium, magnesium, potassium and iodine and thus has wide industrial applications. It was used for glazing pottery, making glass and soap, bleaching and dyeing. It also had applications in the chemical industry, in photography and in medicine (iodine).

About a half-dozen seaweed types, but mainly broad-fronded *Laminaria* species (Oarweed, Tangleweed, *Coirleach*), growing below low-tide level were used to make kelp. Three *Laminaria* species are common on Irish shores, forming large forests in deeper water. They have tough hold-fasts, flexible stipes (Sea Rod, *Slat Mara*) and broad blades (Oarweed) divided into strap-like fronds.[5.5] The kelp was washed up in spring storms or cut during low spring tides. Sickles or special long-handled rakes or hooks (*crúca* or *racán*) were used to tear it off the rocks, while a type of pitchfork was used to gather loose material. The areas harvested would regrow each year.

Ó Concheanainn (1993) describes kelp making in Inis Meáin in the early twentieth century. The seaweed was collected from May to August and spread out to dry. From late summer to autumn the dried weed was burned in a stone-lined trough (*tornóg*) on the foreshore. This formed a molten mass which solidified on cooling. Five tonnes of dried seaweed yielded about one tonne of the calcined ash. At its peak, the industry

5.5 Oarweed; 5.6 Former kelp factory and store (An Teach Mór), Port Chorrúch, Inis Mór

exported about 750 tonnes of burnt kelp per annum from the islands for further processing.

A kelp factory (An Teach Mór)[5.6] was built at Port Chorrúch on Inis Mór in the mid-nineteenth century, near one of the most productive seaweed beaches on the islands. Government-sponsored kelp stores and silos were also built in the 1930s, but were little used. Apart from a minor revival during

World War II, the industry was by then in terminal decline. By the late twentieth century the trade was reduced to exporting only the kelp sea-rods that had been cast up on the shore.[5.7]

EDIBLE SEAWEEDS (SEA-VEGETABLES)

The two best-known edible seaweeds in Aran are the traditional carrageen and dillisk, both of which grow in the intertidal zones. The new-found Irish interest in foreign and exotic cuisine has had the bonus of increasing appreciation of our native edible seaweeds. Although now promoted as delicatessen or health foods, there is a lingering disdain for them in some coastal areas because of their history as 'famine foods'.

Carrageen. *Carraigín*[5.8]

Carrageen (from the Irish *carraigín*), or Irish moss, includes two red-alga species, *Chondrus crispus* and *Mastocarpus stellatus*. *C. crispus* has branched fan-shaped fronds, varying in colour from dark red to brownish-yellow. It is most often found growing under the shelter of larger brown seaweeds in rock pools in the middle to subtidal zones. After harvesting in late spring or summer it is spread out to dry and bleach. It contains the hydrocolloid carrageenan, useful as a thickening agent for blancmange and other dishes. It has many other food applications and has been used as a folk remedy for many ailments, including coughs and colds (Ó hEithir 1983; Ó Síocháin 1962).

Dillisk. *Palmaria palmata. Duileasc*[5.9]

Dillisk, or dulse (from the Irish *duileasc*), *Palmaria palmata*, is another red alga like carrageen but grows in the deeper waters (lower and subtidal zones) of exposed shores. Its irregularly shaped flat fronds grow on rocks

5.7 Dried Sea Rods, Inis Oírr; 5.8 Carrageen

and other seaweeds and vary in colour from bright to dark red. Some dillisk types can be eaten raw, their taste described by Tim Robinson (1986) as 'deliciously sweet and salty, and then chewy, with a savour fading to rubbery zero'. It was exported from Aran to mainland towns and had a reputation for curing hangovers (Mason 1936); it was also used as a folk remedy for intestinal worms in children (Ó Síocháin 1962) and included in pig feed (Ó Coigligh 1990).

A smaller form of dillisk (*creathnach*) is found growing on mussels (*diúilicíní*), hence its Irish name of *an Chreathnach Dhiúilicíneach*. Leic na Creathnaí on Oileán Dá Bhranóg off Inis Mór is so named for the dense growth of this dillisk there.

Sea Lettuce. *Ulva* spp. *Glasán (Sleabhac)* 5.10
Sea Lettuce is an edible green alga, easily recognizable by its thin bright-green translucent fronds that turn white when dried out on the foreshore. It grows on rocks and on other seaweeds in sheltered parts of the middle tidal zone. It is used in soups, salads and other dishes. In Aran it has been used to cure indigestion (Ó Síocháin 1962).

5.9 Dillisk

5.10 Sea Lettuce

OTHER SEAWEEDS

Thongweed. *Himanthalia elongata. Ríseach (Ruánach)*[5.11]

Thongweed is a brown alga, forming tough leathery masses of whip-like fronds over a metre in length in the lower and subtidal zones. Young Thongweeds are quite different from mature plants, appearing as small (about 20 mm) leathery olive-green 'buttons' growing from the holdfasts attached to the rocks. It was once an important species used for kelp manufacture in Aran.

Ulva. Lineáil Ghorm[5.12]

Ulva (formerly *Enteromorpha*, but recently reclassified on the basis of molecular research) is a green alga that can be seen growing profusely in Aran where fresh water seeps out from the exposed clay wayboard strata on the seashore and on the cliff faces.[2.7] It is adapted to a wide range of salinities and its striking bright-green colour and lush growth are unmistakable. In hot weather it may dry out, becoming bleached and pure white in colour.

5.11 Thongweed; 5.12 Green alga (*Ulva*)

Molluscs (shellfish) and crustaceans

The shellfish and crustacean fauna of Ireland comprise some hundreds of species, many of which are also found in Aran. However, to include them all would be beyond the scope of this *Nature Guide* and therefore only the more obvious ones that visitors to Aran are likely to come across are described.

Most of the rocky shores on the islands are quite exposed, but these are conditions that suit some species, such as mussels and barnacles. Although most of the common shellfish are edible (and delicious), few Irish people bother to collect this free food.

Limpet. *Patella* spp. *Bairneach*[5.13]

The Limpet is common in the mid- to upper zones of rocky shores and is easily recognized by its comparatively large size (up to 7 cm across) and conical shell. When the tide is in they 'graze' on the thin coating of algae and lichens that coat the rocks. They wander slowly over the rocks, often leaving visible traces behind, but usually return to their original positions when the tide falls. The Irish name *Bairneach* can cause some confusion due to its similarity to the English 'Barnacle' (below).

A very small but distinctive limpet, the Blue-rayed Limpet (*Helcion pellucidum*), is found growing, not on rocks, but on kelp seaweeds. It is orange-brown to yellowish in colour, up to 1.5 cm in size, and when young has broken blue iridescent lines running down its translucent shell.

Limpets and periwinkles once formed part of the Aran diet, particularly for the evening meal. It was the custom to bring a live fish into the house

5.13 Limpets and Barnacles

on St Brigid's Day (1 February) to ensure a good fishing season, but limpets and periwinkles could be substituted for 'real' fish (Ó Coigligh 1990).

Barnacle. *Semibalanus (Balanus)* and *Chthamalus* spp. *Giurán (Garbhán Carraige)*[5.13]

Although the barnacle is the same shape as the limpet, and grows alongside it, it is a crustacean (related to crabs) rather than a snail and does not move about. It is much smaller (less than 1 cm across) than the limpet, with the main body comprising six plates. Four smaller plates at the top open to allow the barnacle to feed when the tide is in.

Mussel. *Mytilus edulis.* *Diúilicín*[5.14]

Mussels are edible bivalve (two-shelled) molluscs, dark bluish-black in colour, often forming extensive colonies on exposed rocky shores in Aran. They attach themselves by means of tough threads (byssus) to any solid structures in the mid- to lower zones where there is plenty of water movement. They use their gills to filter out small animals and plants from the seawater.

5.14 Mussels

5.15 Periwinkles

Periwinkle. *Littorina* spp. *Faocha (Gioradán)* [5.15]
Periwinkles are one of the commonest of the winkle family and are found on all types of rocky seashore, often underneath seaweeds. They have thick coiled shells, up to 3 cm long, often showing concentric ridges and dark lines, and varying in colour from dark grey-brown to bright yellow. Archaeological digs show that they have been a food source in Ireland since man first arrived here. The edible species of winkle (*L. littorea*) once featured in the Aran diet but is now usually only harvested for export.

Dogwhelk. *Nucella lapillus. Cuachma Chon* [5.16]
The Dogwhelk is a common sea snail, somewhat larger (up to 4 cm long) than periwinkle, and usually white to light brown in colour. In contrast to most other shellfish it is carnivorous rather than herbivorous. It feeds on other sea animals, often indicated by the empty shells of barnacles and mussels in its vicinity.

5.16 Dogwhelks; 5.17 Beadlet Anemone

Cnidarians (Actiniaria)

Sea anemones. *Bundún*

Sea anemones and jellyfish belong to the group of 'jelly animals' known as cnidarians. The anemones are usually found as single polyps, 2–15 cm in diameter, mostly reddish in colour, on rocks and in pools in the middle to subtidal zones. Their tentacles contain stinging cells to capture minute marine organisms. The tentacles are withdrawn to avoid desiccation when exposed at low tide, or when they are disturbed, whereupon the anemones become small jelly-like blobs.

Six of the anemone species recorded in Ireland are found in Aran. The most common species are the Beadlet Anemone[5.17] (*Actinia equina*) and the Dahlia Anemone (*Urticina felina*).

Farming

6

Among these stones is very sweet pasture, so that beefe, veal, mutton are better and earlyer in season here, then elsewhere and of late, there is plenty of cheese and tillage

Roderic O'Flaherty, 1684

… we entred into the Barony of Burren, of which it is said, that it is a country where there is not water enough to drown a man, wood enough to hang one, nor earth enough to bury him; which last is so scarce, that the inhabitants steal it from one another, and yet their cattle are very fat; for the grass growing in turfs of earth, of two or three foot square, that lie between the rocks, which are of limestone, is very sweet and nourishing.

General Edmund Ludlow, 1651

Farming system

The National Soil Survey of Ireland (1980) describes the Aran and Burren soils as 'rendzinas with outcropping rock' and bluntly classifies them as 'extremely limited' for agriculture. The expanses of outcropping rock are clearly visible in the satellite image of the area.[1.1] Only about a third of the land can be utilized for grazing and less than a tenth for cultivation. The maze of small fields,[6.1] individually named and numbering 14,000 on Inis Mór alone (Robinson 1995), is more typical of the nineteenth century and what are classified as the 'more difficult' soils of Ireland. A visitor's first impression is to wonder how any worthwhile farming could be carried out on such a barren landscape.

The Census of Agriculture 2000 recorded 1659 cattle and 285 sheep for the three islands, on a total land area of 4330 hectares. This amounts to less than half a livestock unit per hectare (LU/hectare), which is well below the national average. However, this is compensated to some extent by the superior quality of Aran's young livestock, which has been recognized for centuries (O'Flaherty 1824).

Practically all Aran households own land and are farmers to at least some extent. Many holdings are in elongated strips running across the islands, usually including some foreshore for access to seaweed. The nominal size of a holding (*cnagaire*) that was regarded as providing for the basic needs of one family (cow, calf, horse, sheep, pigs and potatoes) is about 6.5 hectares (16 acres). Commercial farming, such as significant cattle rearing for sale, would require additional land.

The Irish Land Commission bought out the Aran landlords in 1922 and distributed the land, in small lots of 10–20 hectares, to the former tenants. In contrast to the mainland, there were no large estates to be broken up and added to uneconomic holdings. Despite some consolidation and 'striping' by the Land Commission to form more regular holdings, most farms are still small and fragmented. In the absence of any extra land to redistribute, the Land Commission's predecessor in such matters, the Congested Districts Board, had promoted alternative enterprises such as land reclamation, crafts and fishing.

Livestock production (mainly drystock/suckler cattle and sheep[6.2]) is the principal farming enterprise in Aran, with most young animals being exported for finishing on the mainland. In earlier times horses, and some-

6.1 Field pattern, Inis Meáin

times cattle, were moved to Connemara during summer droughts (transhumance). Conversely, Connemara cattle for fattening (*slóchtaí*) were transported to the islands at certain times of the year to avail of the 'sweeter' grazing conditions there.

The cattle production system is unique in that the mild climate and soil conditions allow most animals to be out-wintered, with some supplementary feeding of hay or fodder roots. The thousands of small, fragmented and irregularly shaped fields make the mechanized silage-based winter feeding system of the mainland impracticable. Hay[6.3] is made in the traditional manner, but with the motorized strimmer now replacing the scythe.

The mean January temperature[2.1] is above 6°C, the minimum temperature for grass growth. The limestone bedrock acts as a giant storage heater, absorbing heat in the summer and releasing it in the winter. It also absorbs whatever meagre sunshine occurs in winter. Thus grass continues to grow year-round, except during the very occasional frosty spells or when gale-driven salt spray scorches the leaves. Winter and early spring grazing limits both scrub invasion and grass height. The winter grazing is of particular ecological importance, allowing the unique Burren-type flora to flourish from late spring to summer.

Only hand implements are used for tillage crops, as the fields are too small and stony for machinery. In the nineteenth century, O'Flaherty (1824) noted that the verdant and fertile spots produced good and early crops of oats, barley, wheat, flax and rye. In the first half of the twentieth century potatoes were regularly exported in good (i.e. non-drought) years (Mason 1936). Nowadays, however, potatoes supply only household needs. They are grown in the so-called 'lazy beds',[6.4] a misnomer since this method is quite labour-intensive. The plots are fertilized with black and red seaweeds (*feamainn dhubh* and *feamainn dhearg*), from the upper and lower tidal zones, respectively. In his well-known poem 'An tEarrach Thiar' (The Western Spring, 1949) Máirtín Ó Direáin describes an Aran farmer hauling red seaweed up from the shore in a wicker basket on a bright Spring day:

> *Fear ag caithimh*
> *Cliabh dá dhroim*
> *Is an fheamainn dhearg*
> *Ag lonrú*
> *I dtaitneamh gréine*
> *Ar dhuirling bhán:*
> > *Niamhrach an radharc*
> > *San Earrach thiar*

6.2 Inis Meáin, with Cliffs of Moher in distance. The Aran farming system maintains a species-rich flora in the pastures

6.3 Saving the hay, Inis Meáin

6.4 Roger and Colm Faherty planting potatoes on Inis Meáin. Seaweed fertilizer, right foreground

Rye still supplies straw for the few remaining thatched houses, forage for livestock and some grain for poultry.[6.5] It is a particularly tall cereal (up to 1.5m) but the high stone walls protect it from wind-throw. Andy Bleasdale studied the history, distribution and ecology of rye in Aran in the early 1990s.

To increase or replace the meagre income from cattle rearing, some alternative farm enterprises have been tried out over the years. Daffodils and tulips were introduced in the 1970s and 1980s. Deer breeding stock and goats have also been evaluated. Lucerne (Alfalfa, *Medicago sativa*), a drought-resistant forage species, was introduced in the late nineteenth century. It continues to thrive in the sandy coastal areas (machairs, see pp. 74–5) in dry summers when grass growth has practically ceased.[6.6]

6.5 Rye, Inis Meáin; 6.6 Lucerne, Inis Meáin

The soils

The Aran landscape is a 'glaciated karst' (Chapter 2). Far from being 'natural', its current appearance reflects the cumulative influence of climatic changes since the end of the last Ice Age (8000 BC) and of farming practices since the Neolithic Age (4000–2000 BC). For this reason, our understanding and appreciation of the unique Aran environment is incomplete unless farming practices are also taken into account. A farming/environmental balance has evolved over time, but this balance is continuously under threat by changes in the wider agricultural economy that affect land-use.

There is evidence that Aran and The Burren had a mineral soil cover in the post-Ice Age period. Pollen analysis of lake sediments from An Loch Mór on Inis Oírr shows that woodland predominated about 4000 BC. Neolithic and Bronze Age (2000–600 BC) farmers then gradually cleared the woodlands for cultivation. The farming system, coupled with periodic climatic deterioration, hastened erosion. In some places the elaborate stone walls traverse large tracts of completely bare limestone, suggesting that such areas may once have had land worth enclosing.

Usable farmland in Aran is confined mainly to machairs and rendzina-type soils. In rendzinas, the topsoil (A horizon) rests directly on the parent material (C horizon, limestone rock in this case), with no intervening sub-soil (B horizon). These rendzinas are skeletal (usually less than 5 cm deep), dark, free-draining organic soils derived from the weathering of limestone-based material over thousands of years. Although classified as 'extremely limited' for agriculture, nevertheless their structure and the Aran climate make them particularly well-suited for out-wintering livestock. The sparse soil resists water-logging and poaching by animals' hooves and, together with the shelter of the high stone walls, provides a relatively warm and dry 'lie' for out-wintered cattle. They are heavily leached and are thus nutrient-poor. However, species that can tolerate low-nutrient stresses, such as the unique Burren/Aran flora, flourish in such conditions.[6.2]

In addition to the natural machairs and rendzinas, man-made soils (*garraithe* or gardens) are a feature of the Aran landscape. These have often been described in books and films about the islands. Over the centuries, the islanders filled the grykes with stones and broke up the bare limestone pavements (*ag stocáil*), overlaying them with sand, seaweed and animal manure. In time, this formed a fertile plaggen soil[6.7] with rotations of

6.7 Man-made field overlying rock, Inis Meáin

potatoes, vegetables, rye and pasture. In earlier times, farmers were known to scavenge the precious soil accumulating under the stone walls by knocking and rebuilding them. Roadside soil and the loose clay wayboards underneath the limestone terraces (a 'fossil soil', p. 11) would also be scraped out and spread on the fields. Such labour-intensive practices have now largely died out.

REPS

Since the 1970s the Aran Islands, as part of The Burren, have come under an ever-evolving succession of national and EU environmental designations. These include ASIs (Areas of Scientific Interest), ESAs (Environmentally Sensitive Areas), NHAs (Natural Heritage Areas), SACs (Special Areas of Conservation), and Habitat Directives. These have all affected farming practices on the islands. Currently, more than half (mostly the southern and south-western parts) of the three islands are in SACs, containing various habitats listed in Annex 1 of the EU Habitats Directive.

REPS (Rural Environment Protection Scheme)[6.8] is the overall farm scheme that takes all current environmental designations into account.

140

Practically all Aran landowners participate in REPS, the main objectives of which are:

1. Farming practices and production sympathetic to conservation and environment
2. Protection of wildlife habitats and endangered plants and animals
3. Production of quality food in an environmentally friendly way

REPS has undoubtedly improved the visual aspects of Aran farming. Abandoned equipment and vehicles have been cleared away. The proper maintenance of the magnificent stone walls,[6.1] [6.2] extending for more than 2400 km (Robinson 1995), comes under a particular REPS measure. The traditional field entrance of a pile of rounded stones (*bearna*), knocked down and rebuilt sometimes daily, is now replaced by a proper galvanized gate

6.8 REPS course, Inis Meáin, 2003: farmers identifying Purple Milk-vetch, a Protected Species (inset). Standing, left to right: Taimín Mhéine (Ó Conghaile), Máirtín Mháirt (Ó Culáin), Seáinín Peadar Máirtín (Flatharta), Pádraic Seán Colm (Mac Donnacha), Pádraic Coisdealbha, Beartla Micil Máirín (Ó Conghaile), Mícheál O'Flaherty (Teagasc Advisor), Ciarán Mhéine (Ó Fatharta), Seáinin Seán Beartla (Ó Fatharta). Kneeling, left to right: Ruairí Roger (Ó Concheanainn), Dara Beag (Ó Fatharta), Pádraic Taimín (Ó Meachair)

(somewhat to the dismay of nostalgic visitors). Cattle crushes have been installed on holdings for livestock inspection and treatment.

Limitation of groundwater pollution is also an important component of REPS and is particularly relevant to the free-draining karstic soils of Aran and The Burren. The scheme therefore controls fertilizer and slurry spreading rates and the location of animal feeding sites.

The future

Recent reforms of the EU Common Agricultural Policy (CAP), WTO agreements and EU enlargement will affect Aran farmers as much as those on the mainland. The European taxpayer had become increasingly unwilling to support guaranteed prices for unlimited agricultural production, export subsidies that impoverished Third-World farmers, and the environmental costs of intensive systems. The main reforms are that farm supports are now 'decoupled' from production and replaced by area-based direct payments, and that farm output is now more market-led. In addition, agricultural supports are being integrated with wider environmental and rural development policies. Quite apart from the CAP and the WTO, the overall European trend towards specialization and intensification on the better land, and part-time farming, marginalization and even abandonment of poorer land will also influence Aran farming.

Farming in Aran has declined in importance relative to fishing and tourism, and the *garraithe* that supplied household needs are disappearing. This reduces the rich variety of the landscape and consequently also reduces the range of wild flora and fauna species. Abandonment of fields in Aran would result in invasion by scrub, as is already happening in parts of the Burren karst in County Clare and in the Slovenian region from where the term 'karst' originated.

Despite its decreased importance, farming still comprises an integral part of Aran's varied landscape and economy. Survival of Aran's unique Burren-type flora, in particular, depends on maintaining the traditional low-intensity farming practices that have evolved over centuries (Dunford 2002). Therefore, all the various environmental measures, and REPS in particular, should be designed to reward Aran farmers as custodians of their unique natural environment. On the other hand, subsidizing farmers to persist with old-fashioned husbandry runs the risk of turning the islands into a folk park.

A very welcome development in 2005 was the launch of the EU-supported BurrenLIFE Project. This aims to maintain the traditional farming/environment balance of the region and to increase public understanding of the management of such areas of high environmental value. There are also proposals to expand the current National Park in south-east Clare to cover the entire Burren. The remit of both the BurrenLIFE and the National Park proposals could be usefully extended to include the Aran Islands.

Up to now, farmers have not been the prime beneficiaries of the type of tourism (eco-tourism) that Aran's unique landscape attracts. A sensitive and coordinated development of the farming, natural environment and tourism sectors of the Aran economy is required, to the mutual and long-term sustainability of each sector.

Bibliography

Andrews, W. 1845. 'Observations on the botany of Great Arran Island, Galway Bay, made during an excursion thither in August and September 1845'. *The London Journal of Botany* 4: 569–70.

Ár nOileán, Tuile 's Trá. 2003. *Mná Fiontracha*. Bailiúchán Bhéaloideas Árann. ISBN 0 9546061 1 6.

Bassett, J.A. & Curtis, T.G.F. 1985. 'The nature and occurrence of sand-dune machair in Ireland'. *Proceedings of the Royal Irish Academy* 85B: 1–20.

Betjeman, J. 1958. *John Betjeman's Collected Poems*. John Murray, London.

Bleasdale, A. 1994. 'The History, Distribution and Ecology of the Rye Crop and its Associated Weed Flora in the Aran Islands, Galway'. Unpublished report, Department of Botany, NUI Galway.

Bond, K. (NUI Cork). 2005. Personal communication.

Breen, J. (NUI Limerick). 2004. Personal communication.

Bullock, I.D., Drewett, D.R. & Mickleburgh, S.P. 1983. 'The chough in Ireland'. *Irish Birds* 2: 257–71.

Cabot, D. 1999. *Ireland – A Natural History*. HarperCollins, London. ISBN 000 220079 1.

Challinor, H., Murphy Wickens, S., Clark, J. & Murphy, A. 1999. *A Beginner's Guide to Ireland's Seashore*. Sherkin Island Marine Station. ISBN 1 87 049296 X.

Chinery, M. 2004. *Butterflies*. HarperCollins, Glasgow. ISBN 0 00 717852 2.

Colgan, N. 1893. 'Notes on the flora of the Aran Islands'. *The Irish Naturalist* 2: 75–8, 106–11.

Cooper, D. 1977. *Hebridean Connection*. Routledge & Kegan Paul, London. ISBN 0 7100 8484 6.

Curtis, T.G.F. & McGough, H.N. 1988. *The Irish Red Data Book*. Government Publications, Dublin. ISBN 0 7076 0032 4.

Curtis, T.G.F., McGough, H.N. & Wymer, E.D. 1988. 'The discovery and ecology of rare and threatened arable weeds, previously considered extinct in Ireland, on the Aran Islands, County Galway'. *Irish Naturalists' Journal* 22 (12): 505–12.

Daly, D., *et al.* (eds). 2000. *The Karst of Ireland*. Karst Working Group, Geological Survey of Ireland. ISBN 1 899702 41 5.

Daly, E.P. 1977. 'A hydrogeological investigation on Inishmaan, Aran Islands'. Internal Report No. 3, Ground Water Division, Geological Survey of Ireland.

D'Arcy, G. 1981. *The Guide to the Birds of Ireland*. Irish Wildlife Publications, Dublin. ISBN 0 9507842 0 6.

D'Arcy, G. 1994. 'The Wildlife of the Aran Islands' in Waddell, J. *et al.* (eds). *The Book of Aran*, pages 57–70.

D'Arcy, G. & Hayward, J. 1992. *The Natural History of The Burren*. Immel Publishing, London. ISBN 0 907151 64 7.

de Buitléar, É. (ed.). *Wild Ireland*. Amach Faoin Aer Publishing, Dublin. ISBN 0 94172 03 X.

de Valéra, M. 1958. *A Topographical Guide to the Seaweeds of Galway Bay*. Institute for Industrial Research and Standards, Dublin.

Dempsey, E. & O'Clery, M. 1993. *The Complete Guide to Ireland's Birds*. Gill & Macmillan, Dublin. ISBN 0 7171 1973 4.

Doyle, G. 1993. '*Cuscuta epithymum* (L.) L. (Convolvulaceae), its hosts and associated vegetation in a limestone pavement habitat in The Burren Lowlands in County Clare (H9), Western Ireland'. *Biology and Environment* 93B: 61–7.

Dunford, B. 2002. *Farming and The Burren*. Teagasc, Dublin. ISBN 1 84170 321 4.

Fairley, J.S. 1975. *An Irish Beast Book – a natural history of Ireland's furred wildlife*. Blackstaff Press, Belfast. ISBN 85640 090 4.

Feehan, J. 1994. 'The Geology of the Aran Islands' in Waddell, J. *et al.* (eds). *The Book of Aran*, pages 17–34.

Firth, C.H. (ed.). 1894. *The Memoirs of Edmund Ludlow*. Clarendon Press, Oxford. Volume 1, p. 292.

Forey, P. & Lindsay, R. 1997. *Luibheanna Leighis*. An Gúm, Baile Átha Cliath. ISBN 1 85791 216 0.

Gray, N., Thomas, G., Trewby, M. & Newton, S.F. 2003. 'The status and distribution of Choughs *Pyrrhocorax pyrrhocorax* in the Republic of Ireland, 2002/2003'. *Irish Birds* 7 (2): 147–56. ISSN 0332 0111.

Haddon, A.C. 1893. 'The Aran Islands, County Galway: A Study of Irish Ethnography'. *The Irish Naturalist* 2 (12): 303–8.

Hannon, C., Berrow, S.D. & Newton, S.F. 1998. 'The status and distribution of breeding Sandwich *Sterna sandvicensis*, Roseate *S. dougallii*, Common *S. hirundo*, Arctic *S. paradisaea* and Little Terns *S. albifrons* in Ireland 1995'. *Irish Birds* 6 (1): 1–22.

Hart, H.C. 1875. *A list of plants found in the islands of Aran, Galway Bay*. Hodges, Foster & Co., Dublin.

Heaney, S. 1966. 'Lovers on Aran' in *Death of a Naturalist*. Faber & Faber, London.

Holland, C.H. (ed.). 2001. *The Geology of Ireland*. Dunedin Academic Press, Edinburgh. ISBN 1 903765 07 2.

How, W. 1650. *Phytologia Britannica*. London.

Hutchinson, C. 1986. *Watching Birds in Ireland*. Country House, Dublin. ISBN 0 946172 08 0.

Keane, T. & Collins, J.F. (eds). 2004. *Climate, Weather and Irish Agriculture* (2nd edn). AGMET Group, Met Éireann and NUI Dublin. ISBN 0 9511551 9 9.

Kingston, S., O'Connell, M. & Fairley, J.S. 1999. 'Diet of otters *Lutra lutra* on Inishmore, Aran Islands, west coast of Ireland'. *Biology and Environment: Proceedings of the Royal Irish Academy* 99B (3): 173–82.

Lansdown, R. 1994. *Ireland's Bird Life – a world of beauty*. M. & S. Murphy (eds). Sherkin Island Marine Station. ISBN 1 870492 80 3.

Lewis, S. 1837. *A Topographical Dictionary of Ireland*. S Lewis & Co., London. Volume 1, pages 76–8. Also reprinted in B. & R. Ó hEithir (eds). *An Aran Reader*, pages 18–28.

Lhwyd, E. 1712. 'Some farther observations relating to the antiquities and natural history of Ireland'. *Philosophical Transactions of the Royal Society of London* 27: 524–6.

Ludlow, G.E. 1651. *See* Firth, C.H.

Lysaght, L. 2002. *An Atlas of Breeding Birds of The Burren and the Aran Islands*. BirdWatch Ireland. ISBN 1 899204 15 6.

McCarthy, P.M. & Mitchell, M.E. 1988. *Lichens of The Burren Hills and the Aran Islands*. Officina Typographica, Galway. ISBN 0 907775 20 9.

McGrath, D. 1984. 'The Seashore' in É. de Buitléar (ed.). *Wild Ireland*, pages 96–121.

Mac an Iomaire. S. 1985. *Cladaí Chonamara*. An Gúm, Baile Átha Cliath. First published in 1938.

Mason, T.H. 1936. *The Islands of Ireland*. B.T. Batsford, London.

Mathews, A.C. 1983. *Minding Ruth*. The Gallery Press, Dublin. ISBN 0 904011 39 9.

Merriman, B. 1982. *Cúirt an Mheon-Oíche*. An Clóchomhar Tta, Baile Átha Cliath.

Mitchell, F. 1990. *The Way That I Followed – A Naturalist's Journey around Ireland*. Country House, Dublin. ISBN 0 946172 21 8.

Moore, D. 1854. 'Notes on some rare Plants, including *Ajuga pyramidalis*, in Arran'. *The Phytologist* 5: 189–91.

Morrissey, J., Kraan, S. & Guiry, M.D. 2001. *A Guide to Commercially Important Seaweeds on the Irish Coast*. Bord Iascaigh Mhara.

National Soil Survey of Ireland. 1980. *Ireland, General Soil Map* (2nd edn). An Foras Talúntais, Dublin.

Nelson, E.C. 1997. *The Burren – a companion to the wildflowers of an Irish limestone wilderness*. Sampton, Dublin. ISBN 1 898706 10 7.

Nelson, E.C. 1999. *Wild plants of The Burren and the Aran Islands*. The Collins Press, Cork. ISBN 1 898256 70 5.

Nelson, E.C. & Walsh, W.F. 1993. *Trees of Ireland: Native and Naturalized*. The Lilliput Press, Dublin. ISBN 1 874675 24 4.

Ní Nuadháin, M. 1992. *Cois Trá*. An Gúm, Baile Átha Cliath.

Nowers, J.E. & Wells, J.G. 1892. 'The plants of the Aran Islands, Galway Bay'. *Journal of Botany, London* 30: 180–83.

Ó Coigligh, C. 1990. *Seanchas Inis Meáin*. Coiscéim, Baile Átha Cliat.

Ó Concheanainn, P. 1993. *Inis Meáin – Seanchas agus Scéalta*. An Gúm, Baile Átha Cliath. ISBN 1 85791 054 0. First published in 1931.

Ó Díreáin, M. 1996. *Dánta 1939–1979*. An Clóchomhar Tta, Baile Átha Cliath.

O'Donovan, J. 1839. 'Ordnance Survey Letters: County Galway'. Typescript copy (1928) of manuscript original, Royal Irish Academy. Volume 3.

Ó hEithir, B. & R. (eds). 1991. *An Aran Reader*. The Lilliput Press, Dublin. ISBN 0 946640 54 8.

Ó hEithir, R. 1983. 'Folk Medical Beliefs and Practices in the Aran Islands, County Galway'. MA thesis, University College Dublin.

O'Flaherty, J.T. 1824. 'A sketch of the history and antiquities of the southern islands of Aran, lying off the West coast of Ireland'. *Transactions of the Royal Irish Academy* 14: 79–140.

O'Flaherty, R. 1684. *A Chorographical Description of West or H-Iar Connaught*. Written (but not then published) for the Dublin Philosophical Society. Edited by James Hardiman, 1846, for the Irish Archaeological Society. Facsimile reprint, 1978, Kenny's Bookshop and Art Galleries, Galway. Parts reprinted in B. & R. Ó hEithir (eds). *An Aran Reader*, pages 15–17.

O'Flaherty, T. 1991. 'Netting Guillemots' in B. & R. Ó hEithir (eds). *An Aran Reader*, pages 183–8.

O'Gorman, F. (ed.). 1979. *The Irish Wildlife Book*. John Coughlan, Dublin.

Ó Síocháin, P.A. 1962. *Aran, Isles of Legend*. Foilsiúcháin Éireann, Baile Átha Cliath.

Ogilby, L. 1845. 'Notes of a Botanical Ramble in Connemara and Arran'. *The Phytologist* 2: 345–51.

Oifig an tSoláthair, Baile Átha Cliath. 1978. *Ainmneacha Plandaí agus Ainmhithe – Flora and Fauna Nomenclature.*

Pochin Mould, D.D.C. 1972. *The Aran Islands*. David & Charles, Newton Abbot. ISBN 0 7153 5782 4.

Powell, A. 1984. *Oileáin Árann*. Wolfhound Press, Dublin. ISBN 0 905473 81 7.

Pracht, M., *et al.* 2004. *Geology of Galway Bay. A geological description to accompany the Bedrock Geology 1:100,000 Scale Map series, Sheet 14, Galway Bay.* Geological Survey of Ireland. ISBN 1 899702 46 6.

Praeger, R.L. 1895. 'Notes on the flora of Aranmore'. *The Irish Naturalist* 4: 249–52.

Reynolds, J. 1983. ' "Algal paper" on Inishmore, Aran Islands, Co Galway'. *Irish Naturalists' Journal* 21 (1): 50.

Robinson, T. 1986. *Stones of Aran: Pilgrimage*. Penguin Books, London. ISBN 0 14 011565 X.

Robinson, T. 1995. *Stones of Aran: Labyrinth*. The Lilliput Press, Dublin. ISBN 1 874675 50 3.

Robinson, T. 1996. *Oileáin Árann, a companion to the map of the Aran Islands.* Folding Landscapes. ISBN 0 9504002 7 0.

Rohan, P.K. 1975. *The Climate of Ireland*. The Stationery Office, Dublin.

Scannell, M.J.P. 1972. ' "Algal paper" of *Oedogonium* sp., its occurrence in The Burren, County Clare'. *Irish Naturalists' Journal* 17 (5): 147–52.

Scannell, M.J.P. & Jebb, M.H.P. 2000. 'Flora of Connemara and The Burren – Records from 1984'. *Glasra* 4: 7–45.

Scannell, M.J.P. & Synnott, D.M. 1987. 'Census Catalogue of the Flora of Ireland'. The Stationery Office, Dublin.

Sharrock, J.T.R. 1976. *The Atlas of Breeding Birds in Britain and Ireland*. British Trust for Ornithology and Irish Wildbird Conservancy. ISBN 0 903793 01 6.

Spellissy, S. 2003. *Window on Aran*. The Book Gallery, Ennis. ISBN 0 9545218 0 3.

Stace, C. 1997. *New Flora of the British Isles* (2nd edn). Cambridge University Press. ISBN 0 521 58933 5.

Stationery Office, Dublin. 1996. *Report on the Interdepartmental Co-ordinating*

Committee on Island Development: A Strategic Framework for Developing the Offshore Islands of Ireland. ISBN 0 707623510.

Stelfox, A.W. 1933. 'On the occurrence of a peculiar race of the humble bee, *Bombus smithianus* White, on the Aran Islands in Western Ireland'. *Irish Naturalists' Journal* 4: 235–8.

Sterry, P. 2004. *Complete Irish Wildlife*. HarperCollins, London. ISBN 0 00 717629 5.

Synge, J.M. 1907. *The Aran Islands*. Maunsel & Co., Dublin. Reprinted in 1988 by Blackstaff Press, Belfast. ISBN 0 856404128.

Synge, J.M. 1992. *Plays, Poems and Prose*. J.M. Dent & Sons, London. First published in 1941. ISBN 0 460 87070 X.

Waddell, J. *et al.* (eds). 1994. *The Book of Aran*. Tír Eolas, Galway. ISBN 1 873821 03 4.

Webb, D.A. 1980. 'The Flora of the Aran Islands'. *Journal of Life Sciences, Royal Dublin Society* 2 (1): 51–83.

Webb, D.A. 1983. 'The flora of Ireland in its European context'. *Journal of Life Sciences, Royal Dublin Society* 4 (2): 143–60.

Webb, D.A., Parnell, J. & Doogue, D. 1996. *An Irish Flora* (7th edn). Dundalgan Press, Dundalk. ISBN 0 85221 131 7.

Webb, D.A. & Scannell, M.J.P. 1983. *Flora of Connemara and The Burren*. Royal Dublin Society and Cambridge University Press. ISBN 0 521 23395 X.

Whilde, A. 1993. *Threatened mammals, birds, amphibians and fish in Ireland. The Irish Red Data Book 2: Vertebrates*. HMSO, Belfast.

Williams, N. 1993. *Díolaim Luibheanna*. Sáirséal – Ó Marcaigh, Baile Átha Cliath. ISBN 0 86289069 1.

Wright, E.P. 1866. 'Notes on the Flora of the Islands of Arran, West of Ireland'. *Proceedings of the Natural History Society of Dublin* 5: 96–106.

Wright, E.P. 1867. 'Notes of a botanical tour to the islands of Arran, County Galway'. *Journal of Botany, London* 5: 50–1.

Indexes

Flora and Fauna Index
English Names

Irish Index

General Index: English

A

AlgaeBase 118
alginates 118
alginic acid 118
aphrodisiacs 59
Arctic–Alpine 33, 36, 41, 42, 44, 62
Areas of Scientific Interest (ASIs) 3, 140
Arramara Teoranta 118, 120
aspirin 53, 68

B

baskets 68, 135
Bealtaine festival 64
'Big Bang' 10
bio-indicators 82
block beaches, *see* storm beaches
Bonnie Prince Charlie 78
Botanic Gardens 33, 34, 35
boulder clay 10, 20, 37, 55
Bronze Age 4, 36, 139
Burren, The 4, 9–10, 33
BurrenLIFE Project 143

C

calcicole 40, 49, 62
calcifuge 20, 36, 55, 84
calcite 14, 15
calcium bicarbonate 15
calcium carbonate 9, 14, 83
carbon dioxide 14–15
carbonic acid 14–15, 55
Carboniferous Period 9–11, 16
carrageenan 123
Celtic 5

chert 14
clay wayboards 11, 16, 17, 125, 140
Cliffs of Moher 12, 135
clints 12–16, 23, 33, 37, 41, 81, 83, 84
Common Agricultural Policy (CAP)
    142
Congested Districts Board 17, 29, 133
conglomerate 19
culinary plants 49, 57, 59, 64, 79

D

Department of Agriculture 17
desalination 17
DNA 5
dolomite 9
drought 29, 37, 74, 84, 134, 135, 137
Druids 53
dunes, *see* sand dunes

E

earthquake 28
Enterprise Ireland 117, 118
Environmentally Sensitive Areas (ESAs)
    140
Eriskay (Scotland) 78, 79
erratics, *see* glacial erratics
ethnobotany 38

F

feldspar 83
fodder roots 24, 134
foraminifera 16
fossils 10, 12, 16, 17
    f. soil 11, 140

G

Gaelic Revival 4

Notes

Notes

Notes

Notes

Notes

Notes